Control Your Difficult Divorce

ASHLEY & CHRISTOPHER BRUCE

CONTROL YOUR DIFFICULT DIVORCE
Copyright © 2021 by Ashley & Christopher Bruce
All rights reserved.

This book or any portion thereof may not be reproduced or used in any manner whatsoever without the express written permission of the author except for the use of brief quotations in a book review.

Printed in the United States of America
First Printing, 2017

ISBN: 978-0-9975316-1-9

Ashley & Christopher Bruce
1601 Forum Place
Suite 1101
West Palm Beach, Florida 33401
12008 Southshore Blvd, Suite 104
Wellington, Florida, 33414
www.BrucePA.com

ACKNOWLEDGEMENTS

Thank you to our parents, Chrissy, Bernice, Russell, Spencer and Gernot. Your continued love, guidance, and encouragement makes us the world's luckiest children and has put us in the position of accomplishing anything we set our mind to achieving.

We are also especially grateful to those in the mental health profession who have trusted the attorneys of the Bruce Law Firm to help meet the marital and family law needs of their clients, while also helping our law firm's clients move on from the difficult experience of divorce (and sometimes avoid divorce completely through couple's therapy).

LEGAL DISCLAIMER

This book is about divorce planning and strategy and is not a legal treatise or dictionary. There are many lawyers, books and seminars which do an outstanding job explaining the numerous important intricacies of your state or country's divorce laws. Our advice is to hire a competent and ethical divorce lawyer to help you understand how the laws of your state or country apply to your specific situation and to help refine the goals and strategies we tell you to implement in this book. The explanations about divorce law and strategy in this book are not a substitute for hiring a competent divorce lawyer, which is what we recommend you do.

TABLE OF CONTENTS

INTRODUCTION i
    What is the Best Divorce? i
    Other Resources Designed to Help You v

Section 1: Get Your Act Together 1
    Realize There Is No Such Thing as a 3
    "Divorce Miracle" 3
    You Are Part of the Problem 6
    Define Your "Best Life" 11
    Make Time for Yourself 15
    Take Care of Your Physical & Emotional Health 19
    Get Your Act Together Before You Go Any Further 24

Section 2: Learn the Basics of Leverage & Strategy 27
    Your Divorce Strategy is the Most Important Thing Besides You 29
    How People Make Decisions in a Complex Divorce 33
    The First Mover Advantage 38
    (Move First, Unannounced, and Don't Back Off) 38
    Do Not Create Short Term Cash Flow Problems 43
    Be the One to Control the Money & Documents 49
    Being a Nice-Guy or Gal 54
    Will Not Get Your Family Back 54
    Guilty Conscience Agreements 59
    & Exposing Their Secrets 59
    Bringing Their Extra-Marital Relationships to Light (and Keeping Yours in the Dark) 66

Top Five Other "Should Be Obvious" Mistakes to Avoid 71

Section 3: Finalize Your Best Divorce & Best Life Strategies 77

Best Divorce & Best Life Strategy Overview 79

Work with Your Lawyer & Therapist to Refine Your Goals 81

Develop Your Strategy 86

Understand the Timeline of What Will Likely Happen & When 92

Understand Uncertainties & Possible Outcomes.................................94

Section 4: Move Forward & Avoid Distractions 99

Your Life is Now Going to Get Better...101

Finalize Preparations & Avoid Being "Cut Off" 103

How to Tell Your Spouse About the Divorce......................................106

How to Tell Your Children About the Divorce....................................113

Dealing with Family, Friends, & Colleagues 115

Handling Your Spouse During the Divorce..118

Leave the Law to the Lawyer & Focus on Implementing Your Best Life Strategy...123

Avoid Negative Influences 125

When to Reassess Your Best Divorce & Best Life Strategies 126

Section 5: Resolution Focused Litigation.....................................129

Your Litigation Strategy 131

Why Resolution Focused Litigation is Necessary 133

Resolution Focused Litigation Explained 138

The Costs of Delay 144

Utilizing a "Net Expected Value" Settlement Analysis......................147

Section 6: Living Your Best Life After the Divorce......................155

Divorce is Only the Beginning!..157

Best Life Action Items 160

Dealing with Your Former Spouse After the Divorce 166
Stay Out of Divorce Court! 170
Our Other Books Designed to Help You 175
ABOUT THE AUTHORS 177

INTRODUCTION

What is the Best Divorce?

We are divorce lawyers. You'd probably be surprised to know that, despite our profession, we are not personally fans of divorce and everything that comes with it. For this reason, we created the website www.StayMarriedFlorida.com to help people avoid divorce (more on that soon). That said, we believe there is a time and a place for divorce. For some people, the only way to live a happy, healthy and productive life is to end their marriage. These are the people we help in our law practice.

The *Best Divorce* is the one nobody hears about. The *Best Divorce* is settled quickly, on fair terms, without any nastiness, threats, or significant legal fees. Your divorce can be the *Best Divorce*, but it will take some work. Much like the creation of great businesses, investments, or professional practices, the *Best Divorce* will not happen accidentally, easily, or overnight. The *Best Divorce* is the product of purposeful planning followed by executing on strategies designed to produce a specific, desired result. For most people, this result is a clean, favorable, wind up of the legal and family issues involved with divorce and a fresh start in life.

We've written several books on divorce and divorce strategy. These books are available for free download at www.DivorceInformationBooks.com. This particular book focuses on how you can develop a strategy designed for controlling and ending a difficult divorce, on fair terms, as soon as possible. This book was designed for those anticipating a complex divorce. Reading the chapters that follow will be especially helpful for those whose divorce will involve significant financial or reputational matters being "on the line" and for anyone, especially women, who are considering divorce from a narcissistic or emotionally abusive/manipulative spouse.

Throughout this book, we will refer to you living your *Best Life* after your divorce. Your *Best Life* is the life you desire and deserve to have once your divorce is over. It is a life that involves you feeling respected and loved by your friends and family. A life that involves you pursuing your goals and feeling accomplished. A life that is filled with happiness and satisfaction. Your *Best Life* is the life you do not have now but want to be living.

Transitioning from your current life to your *Best Life* is the reason you are seeking a divorce.

This book exists to help you develop and execute strategies for having the *Best Divorce* possible and optimizing your ability to live your *Best Life* after the divorce is over. In this book we'll take you through the main steps involved with developing and executing a *Best Divorce* plan for getting through your divorce with as little collateral damage as possible. We'll help you understand how to do this in a dignified manner that lays the foundation for you living the *Best Life* you desire and deserve after the divorce is over in a manner designed to preserve harmony within your family.

Some of our advice may make you feel like you would be "acting like a different person" or outside of your "comfort zone." If you start to feel this way while reading, we encourage you to think about this: being in your "comfort zone" created part of the situation you are reading this book to fix. You are reading this book to become a "different person." To become different, you have to act different. If you approach ending your marriage in the same way you lived it, you'll be as disappointed in the experience of your divorce as you are with your marriage. Revisit this reality each time you feel like you are being told to act outside of your "comfort zone." Use your divorce as the first opportunity to change for the better and not to continue being miserable or allow others to take advantage of you. Remember, the choice to change to a better life is yours, and yours only.

The bottom line is everything in this book is designed to help you achieve the two goals that we have for all of our clients. The first goal is to help you obtain a divorce on favorable terms as soon as possible. The second goal is to help you lay a foundation for living your ideal life when your divorce is over. If you read this book, and apply our suggestions to your situation, you will give yourself the best opportunity to attain these goals and have the *Best Divorce* possible.

We wish you the best as you begin this challenging but surmountable process.

Ashley & Christopher Bruce
West Palm Beach, Florida

Other Resources Designed to Help You

Before we go any further, we wanted to make a quick mention of resources we've put online to further help you navigate the divorce process. Our law firm's website, **www.BrucePA.com**, has complementary books, seminars, and forums on divorce strategy, law, and procedure. Also, there are several books available for free download at www.DivorceInformationBooks.com. These books are free and include the Women's Guide for Getting Organized for Divorce, How to Divorce Your Controlling, Manipulative, Narcissistic Husband, our Florida Divorce Law Guide, and our guide on How to Find & Hire Your Divorce Lawyer.

Also, because it is our belief that the real best divorce is the divorce that didn't have to happen, the Bruce Law Firm developed and supports www.StayMarriedFlorida.com, a website devoted to helping couples build, have, and keep healthy relationships. The website has articles, podcast interviews, and a growing directory of extremely talented results-driven therapists.

Section 1: Get Your Act Together

Realize There Is No Such Thing as a "Divorce Miracle"

Having the *Best Divorce* starts with you. It will not happen by chance. There are no miracles in divorce court. A judge's signature on a document legally dissolving your marriage, by itself, is not going to instantly make your life better. Similar to building a successful business, investment, or professional practice, you will be disappointed with your divorce and what comes after if you don't take the time to first develop a clear vision of how divorce fits into a comprehensive plan for improving your life.

Many of the world's most successful businesses in their infancy, before they became bestselling brands, were created by their founders to offer products solving specific problems in ways nobody before thought possible. All large companies started as a vision of something great in somebody's head. Sometimes, the vision was thought to be ridiculous. Sometimes the vision was called unattainable. Sometimes, the vision took years to perfect. The challenges to overcome were all different, but there was always a vision that started it all.

The Apple Computer was created to bring personal computing to everyday people. Before Apple, the only people who had personal computers were the ultra-wealthy or the hobbyists who had the ability to assemble and solder keyboards to motherboards. At the time, most of the computers that existed had to be housed in several rooms and cost millions of dollars. In creating Apple, Steve Jobs and Steve Wozniak had a vision of a world where the rest of the world could attain ownership of their own personal computer.

The skeptics thought they were crazy, but Apple's founders knew they were on to something and ignored the criticism. After a great deal of planning, execution, and a little bit of turmoil and competition, Mr. Jobs' and Mr. Wozniak's vision became a reality. Just think: most of the people reading this book are likely doing so from some version of a personal computer. And many of these are Apple products.

Do you think the fate of Apple would have been the same if Apple's founders went into Steve Jobs' parents' garage and started turning wrenches or banging on motherboards without any idea of what they were trying to build? Would they have gotten anywhere if they didn't know, deep down, that they both had a great vision and the belief that they could make it happen?

Fortunately for you, navigating divorce is nowhere near as complex as creating the next microcomputer. However, you are going to struggle during and after the process if you fail to understand, upfront, that you have the ability to control your life. Further, before hiring a lawyer and rushing to the courthouse, you must develop a vision for a better life (which we refer to as the *Best Life*), and why you believe divorce is the way to make it happen.

There are no divorce miracles. A piece of paper from a judge dissolving your marriage will not instantly make your life better. The *Best Divorce* starts with finding the mindset needed to promote change and having at least a basic understanding of the life you want to live. Without developing this confidence and vision, you can get divorced, but you probably will not do so smoothly or with the assurance of knowing the divorce is part of a larger plan for transforming your life into something better that you already have mapped out in your mind.

How do you attain this direction and vision? Keep reading. The rest of *Section#1: Get Your Act Together* covers what you need to know.

**ASHLEY & CHRISTOPHER BRUCE
CONTROL YOUR DIFFICULT DIVORCE**

You Are Part of the Problem

Over the years of being a divorce lawyer, our clients have given us every reason under the sun to justify to us why they want a divorce. Some tell us they need divorce because their spouse ignores them or their relationship is not much different than two ships passing in the night. Others say their spouse smothers them, making it impossible for them to be their own person. In the morning, we'll hear a husband tell us about how he wants out of the marriage because his wife sits at home all day refusing to get a "real job" and in the afternoon, another will tell me divorce is the only answer because his wife is a workaholic who neglects the family, or doesn't want to have a family. Housewives tell us how they suspect an affair because their husband is ignoring them sexually while others complain their spouse is a sex addict. Sometimes, we feel like we've heard it all when it comes to reasons for a breakdown of a marriage but we sleep soundly at night knowing there is always a new story out there for us to hear.

The funny thing about human nature is seldom do people initially realize their role in problem creation. It is a rare day that a person tells us in a client interview how their arrival in our office was the culmination of their own personal, misguided decision-making over the preceding years or decades. People almost always, understandably, blame the other person for the divorce, and are resistant to admitting their role in creating an unhappy marriage.

Is your life currently miserable? Do you feel like your spouse is stealing your happiness; sealing you off from the world; holding you back on life achievements; spending all of your money; ruining your career; polluting your children or grandchildren; fracturing your family; or injecting toxicity into a relationship in ways you never thought possible? Guess what? **You are part of the problem**.

You might not like hearing this, but you are better off grasping reality now. Your life decisions are a great part of why you are in a marriage you think needs to end. Your choices led you to where you are right now. Believe it or not, if you are unhappy, miserable, beaten down, or [insert other description of your life] part of the reason is because *you did it to yourself*.

Before you throw this book or your reading device at the wall and take to vilifying us for being insensitive, chauvinistic, or inhuman, do yourself a favor and read the rest of this chapter. It will make your life better. We promise.

You are not to blame for your spouse's disgraceful, illicit or illegal behavior. You should not feel like you created your spouse's violent acts, chronic addictions, or serial philandering because you are not the one who made the choice to swing that fist, maintain the addiction, or fornicate outside of the marriage. We especially stress towards the women reading this book who have been in long-term abusive relationships that they should not feel like they created the unconscionable behavior of their spouse.

Our point in telling you that "you did it to yourself" is to help you realize that you created the situation of being in a relationship that you are contemplating leaving (or maybe deep down wanting to fix). Rarely anyone in this day and age, in the western world, can say they were actually forced to get married. Nor was it only your spouse that perpetuated the problems that have you at the proverbial "door to divorce." The bottom line is this: part of what led you to where you are today, a life you are not happy with, was a series of conscious decisions made by you. So, that's why you need to realize that *you are part of the problem.* Part of why you are here is because, *you did it to yourself.*

ASHLEY & CHRISTOPHER BRUCE
CONTROL YOUR DIFFICULT DIVORCE

The good news is you also have the ability to make choices that make your life better. Just like you - likely without knowing it – helped create your marital problems and unhappiness, you have the ability to create something better. Coming to the realization that you have the power to change your life is probably the most important thing you can do as part of the divorce process. Part of having the *Best Divorce* is learning that you have, and have always had the power to control your own destiny, and then using that knowledge to create the life you desire and deserve. This knowledge is especially empowering for those who have been beaten down over time by chronically selfish or abusive spouses.

Knowing that you, and only you, ultimately control your life going forward, helps you be in the driver's seat when it comes to the divorce process. When you overcome your doubts that you could have a better life in the future, you will be in a much better mindset when it comes to determining what it is you really want out of the divorce. Further, in future relationships, you will be less prone to the desperate decision-making that can cause you to relapse into the same problems that plagued your first marriage.

Before you go any further, take the time to develop and cope with the understanding that your life decisions helped create the situation you want to fix. Then, do your best to get over what has happened in the past. Realize that you have the absolute ability to control your path to living a happy, healthy and prosperous life. Coming to this realization and understanding, with yourself, might just be the most transforming and worthwhile moment you've ever experienced. Do not neglect this step in the *Best Divorce* process.

If you felt like this chapter was too "touchy feely" for you, or did not present any actionable advice, we'll state things differently and in a language you might understand: You helped cause this mess. Get your head out of the sand, suck it up, and stop blaming others for your problems. Your divorce will be quicker, cost less money, and you'll be better off afterwards. Get it? Got it? Good.

**ASHLEY & CHRISTOPHER BRUCE
CONTROL YOUR DIFFICULT DIVORCE**

Define Your "Best Life"

What would your first questions be to someone asking you to invest your hard earned dollars in their business? If you are like most people, you'd be asking them "what does your business do?" followed by "what are you going to do with my money?" You'd probably run from investing with someone who couldn't give a concise answer to these basic questions. How would you ever make any return on your investment in a company that lacked purpose and direction?

It surprises me to see countless successful business owners and investors approach their divorce without the purpose and vision that would be mandatory in their business or investing endeavors. This is asinine. Having the *Best Divorce* is no different than growing a successful business, professional practice, or philanthropic organization. Your attainment of success will be significantly delayed, more expensive, and possibly never achieved, if you start off without a defined purpose.

You need to define your *Best Life* before you spend any more time contemplating divorce. If you could push a magic button and instantly be "living the dream," what would that be like?

ASHLEY & CHRISTOPHER BRUCE
CONTROL YOUR DIFFICULT DIVORCE

Invest the time going through what we'll call the "Who, What, Where, When, Why and How of Separation and Life Improvement." Before you go any further, you absolutely must be able to answer the following questions:

- Who do you want to be as a person?

- What would it take to make you happier and healthier?

- Where would you be living and what type of people would you surround yourself with?

- Why would this life be better than your life now?

- How is divorce a necessary part of you having this life?

Engaging in this analysis, or something like it, is critical. You must have a picture in your mind of what your *Best Life* will be. Otherwise, you'll lack serious direction in how you move forward, and you will not be making purpose-driven decisions when it comes to handling the legal aspects of your divorce. We doubt you would ever consider investing half of your life savings - which is what many lose in their divorce - in a business, idea, or person, without a compelling reason. Divorce should be no different. You need to know your end game, your big picture purpose, before you begin anything. Divorce, no matter how well done, will disrupt your family, friendships, and finances. It would be a huge shame for you to endure the divorce process and not have a better life to show for it. Do yourself a favor and take the time now to understand what you want out of life when the divorce is done. Taking this step costs nothing but your time and brainpower.

If you have no idea what your *Best Life* should be, it might be a sign that you are living it already and things might not be as bad as they seem. Sometimes, people are stressed out with their job, the death of a family member, or something equally traumatic, and end up believing divorce is the answer to making their life better because it is what they've seen others doing. Don't let yourself be one of these people. Also, determining what your *Best Life* should look like is going to be very difficult if you have spent most of your adult years in a toxic relationship.

If you are having a hard time understanding what your *Best Life* should be or envisioning any other life than the miserable one you are living, you need to spend some time with an experienced therapist. They will help you determine why you are unhappy and whether divorce should be part of the solution. The therapist will help you develop a vision of hope and change, even if your spouse has always held you down. Your health insurance likely covers the therapy expense. Most therapists offer evening appointments to accommodate those who work long hours during the day. If you do not know a therapist, we've listed plenty of the great ones in Florida on StayMarriedFlorida.com.

Once you develop your vision of your *Best Life*, we encourage you to write it down and revisit and refine it often. Later in the book, we'll walk through developing a plan of action to make sure everything you are doing to move forward will be for the purpose of getting you closer to living your *Best Life* as soon as possible.

Make Time for Yourself

A key to having the *Best Divorce* and a better life is to be a bit selfish. Did that get your attention? Before you read any further, please know that we're not suggesting that you start acting like a jerk, ignore the needs and feelings of others, or approach the divorce with an "everything is mine" attitude. However, what you need to do as part of "getting your act together" is learn how to make time for yourself. You are going to need it.

With our law firm, most of our clients or their spouses own or manage a business/corporation or are part of a professional practice in the fields of medicine, financial services, or law. Many of these people are highly functioning and successful people who have mastered both their trade or business and the management of other people. They also share the common trait of being very, very, busy and prioritizing the needs of their company or clients (or children, the case of stay at home spouses) over their personal needs. In divorce cases involving these types of people there is a high, positive correlation between the person's ability to put time aside to focus on their divorce and their overall satisfaction with their divorce.

ASHLEY & CHRISTOPHER BRUCE
CONTROL YOUR DIFFICULT DIVORCE

Stated differently: *you are probably going to get run over in your divorce if you are "too busy" to focus on the preparation and execution of your divorce.*

In our view, it is mandatory to have at least four hours a week to yourself as you prepare for, execute on, and recover from your divorce. Initially, most of this time will be devoted to following the divorce planning initiatives laid out in this book. Later, your time will transition to being spent working with your lawyer, therapist and monitoring the progress of the divorce lawsuit once it is put in motion. Finally, this time will be needed later to help you move on from the divorce and make sure the problems plaguing your marriage are not repeated.

Yes, the purpose of hiring divorce lawyers and other professionals is to handle your divorce for you. These people are paid (and paid well) so that your time can be better spent doing other things. However, outsourcing the preparation and execution of the most important personal and financial transaction in your life can only go so far. You are going to need to be part of the process if you want to create the best probability of efficiently obtaining a favorable resolution to your divorce and putting yourself on the path to the life you desire and deserve after the divorce. Doing this takes time. Your time. Time that needs to come from somewhere.

It is imperative that you figure out now how to make time for yourself. You are either going to have to become better at time management, cut off some non-essential activities, or both. Odds are, if you put into place a few basic productivity measures, you will be able to come up with the few hours a week you need to make the difference in your divorce and everything that comes after.

If you have not already, read the book *Getting Things Done* by David Allen, and *168 Hours* by Laura Vanderkam. Also, you can take a cue from us. We created the extra ten hours a week we needed to keep to an exercise routine and write this book by eliminating unscheduled, non-emergency phone calls, having my emails screened and sorted so that we view them primarily once a day (this is huge), and using project management software (Smartsheet.com is simple and low cost) to keep track of delegated client work. With these measures, we are providing better client service (our firm's top priority) while creating the time to focus on other things important to our personal and professional development.

ASHLEY & CHRISTOPHER BRUCE
CONTROL YOUR DIFFICULT DIVORCE

Creating time for yourself is imperative in preparing for and executing on your divorce. You'll also need time for yourself if you want to be happy and healthy after your divorce is over. Furthermore, there is a decent chance that your inability to manage your schedule to carve out time just for you and your relationship contributed to the failure of your marriage and has wreaked havoc on your physical and emotional health. Do you really want to let that happen again?

The bottom line is that prosperity will come to you in many forms after the divorce if you make it possible now to invest time in yourself. Creating this time is not easy, and takes time to implement and discipline to maintain, but it can be done. Our advice is to start now with developing a plan to make your needs your priority. It is okay to be a little bit selfish every now and then.

Take Care of Your Physical & Emotional Health

I (Chris) hate running. I used to do a lot of it when I was in high school. I had an outstanding coach who taught me a lot about the sport and personal perseverance but the fact is I'd absolutely exert myself in the 5k races to finish "in the back of the pack" of runners. There were no easy miles covered with my shoes. As a result, I really cannot stand hearing marathoners casually brag about "getting in" a ten-mile run before breakfast as they prepare for their next big race. Despite my personal dislike for putting on shoes and pounding the pavement, I'll acknowledge there are a few things to learn from marathon runners that can help you have the *Best Divorce*.

There's a reason why you don't see many four-hundred-pound diabetics, with no prior running experience, finishing marathons the morning after a late night of drinking. In order to accomplish what seems like the insurmountable goal of running a 26.2-mile race, marathoners have to get themselves in optimum physical condition. In addition to all the training, to be successful, they have to follow a strict diet leading up to the race day and do what is necessary to control their other health problems enough to allow them to physically perform.

No, we're not going to tell you that your divorce is as physically exerting as running a marathon or preach to you about joining your local running club (you won't see us there). But, we will tell you that in many ways, your divorce can seem like a marathon in that it will take personal and physical perseverance to get past the finish line without feeling like you are being hauled there on a stretcher. For this reason, we strongly encourage you to get your physical and emotional health under control as part of starting the *Best Divorce* process. If you are "a mess" physically or emotionally, it is going to be close to impossible to have the *Best Divorce*.

Look, you can get through your divorce without lifting a weight or stepping on a treadmill. That said, you are going to be better off if you institute some form of a basic exercise program to at least maintain your physical health and serve as an outlet to shake off stress. You should be able to find three days a week where you can do something physical for thirty or forty-five minutes. If you have not exercised in years, the best thing to do after getting clearance from your doctor is to go join a gym that offers beginners classes. Many of the larger gyms and boutique fitness clubs have classes on anything from yoga and spinning, to Pilates and weightlifting that start as early as 5:00 in the morning and go until 9:00 in the evening. Try to do something that gets your body moving.

Further, if you are worried about being lonely after the divorce, getting involved with a sport or joining a gym (especially the classes) can be a great way to start meeting new people who share the quality of having the discipline to take care of themselves. Many gyms and fitness studios (like CrossFit and Orange Theory Fitness) have their own "culture"/ "following", with members often planning social gatherings and events. Integrating into one of these fitness "communities" (which are often very "beginner friendly") can be great for developing or expanding your social connections, which you will want to have during and after the divorce.

If you have any serious or lingering health problems, you should think hard about addressing them now, before you get too deep in the divorce process. You can and should continue preparing for and planning your divorce as outlined in *Steps #2-7* of this book. However, in many cases, you will not be doing yourself any good to tell your spouse you want a divorce or file the divorce lawsuit before addressing a major medical need. You are not going to be on a level playing field with your spouse if you have to contend with a serious health problem at the same time you are handling your divorce. You should not be recovering from a major surgery or receiving treatment for something serious while you are in the middle of a divorce case. If you have a choice, address the medical issues now and then start the divorce.

Similarly, you have to assess your emotional health before you go too much further. It is common to feel anxious, depressed, or confused when you are considering the end of a relationship. Also, these feelings can serve as the catalyst to exacerbating harmful addictions. Your mental health is serious and cannot be ignored. Our belief is that your mental health is more important than your physical heath when it comes to divorce. Much of what has to be done to have the *Best Divorce* involves making well-reasoned decisions and implementing strategies that require you to be free or nearly free of the emotional hindrances that cloud important decision making. If you do not have a "clear head", you need stop wasting time and go see a therapist. Do it now. Some of the great ones in South Florida are listed at www.StayMarriedFlorida.com.

ASHLEY & CHRISTOPHER BRUCE
CONTROL YOUR DIFFICULT DIVORCE

You can read all the self-help books you want but it is foolish to "self-help" your mental health. Doing so takes longer, will not be as effective as professional assistance, and will likely lead to disaster if your "self-help" includes your favorite narcotic. You need your mental health addressed now. Do not downplay the importance of or delay attention to this, especially if you have depression, an addiction, have been in an abusive relationship, or others tell you that you are "co-dependent."

The bottom line is a crucial component of "getting your act together" and preparing for the *Best Divorce* is getting control of your physical and emotional health. You have a lot coming up between a divorce and the new life that comes after. You do not need to be able to run marathons or meditate daily with Buddhist monks, but if you have severe health problems, addictions, or unaddressed emotional issues, you need to address these issues immediately. Do not wait.

Get Your Act Together Before You Go Any Further

We understand. You are miserable. You want this over. You want this over now, or over yesterday. I get it. I know where you are coming from and what you are dealing with, but you need to listen to me. You need to get your own act together before you go any further or your divorce is going to be a mis-directional disaster that leaves you more miserable than you are you are now with the added treat of losing up to fifty percent of your net worth.

Do you want the *Best Divorce* or a protracted battle that costs half your wealth? If you want to setup the best chance of things going the right way, then you need to stop and "get your act together" now before you go any further. You have to realize that there is no such thing as a "divorce miracle." The laws of human nature will get you nowhere but the same place, unless you choose to change, take the time to define what your ideal life looks like, and understand why you need a divorce to have that life (which might not be the case).

While you are embarking on this personal revolution, you need to start making time for yourself. During your divorce, you will need time to think, plan, react, and reflect. You will be railroaded in your divorce if you fail to rearrange your life to make this time available.

And one more thing. As you finish getting your act together, you need to figure out whatever needs to be figured out about your physical and mental health. If you don't have your head on straight, you are never going to have the wherewithal to develop and adhere to a sound divorce strategy. A strategy would be pointless in the first place, if you die or become disabled before or soon after this is all done.

Getting your act together is half the battle towards improving your life immediately. During the process, you might even find that you've already made your life better and divorce is unnecessary. However, if you know that you must still move away from your marriage, you will be in a dramatically better position to prepare for developing and executing on a *Best Divorce* strategy that gets things over on fair terms as soon as possible, and a *Best Life* strategy that sets you up for the life you desire and deserve after the divorce.

Section 2: Learn the Basics of Leverage & Strategy

Your Divorce Strategy is the Most Important Thing Besides You

We see the divorce process to be very much like having to go to a dentist for a root canal or major surgery. By the time many people get to the dentist, something usually "hurts like hell" to the point of rendering them unable to function or think about anything else. The pain is excruciating, and it also hurts that paying the dentist to fix the problem never seems to be completely covered by health insurance.

If someone were to survey people who are about to experience dental surgery as they walked into their dentist's office, we imagine the consensus would be that most of them are fed up. They want to sit down in the dentist's chair and have their problem fixed. And they want that fix immediately because "it hurts!" They would tell you they don't want their life interrupted by having to mess around, dealing with more pain or wasting more time and money to come back and fix the problem later. We're sure more than a few people would tell the surveyor "stop with the damn questions, get me the dentist, and make him bring his drill!"

Divorce is not much different. It "hurts like hell" and what most people want is to end the pain as soon as possible without wasting time and money. And that should be the goal. The *Best Divorce* strategies we advocate are designed to achieve two important, but limited purposes. Purpose #1 is to resolve your divorce as quickly and efficiently as possible on favorable terms, with as little collateral damage as possible. Purpose #2 is to allow you to move towards your *Best Life* in a dignified manner as soon as possible.

The title of this chapter is "Your Divorce Strategy is the Most Important Thing Besides You" for a reason. It's because it's true. The reason why the basics of divorce strategy and leverage is the first thing covered in this book after a chapter on self-care and direction is because, besides your mindset, health and safety, nothing is more important than your divorce strategy. If you want the *Best Divorce,* you have to understand and follow the basic concepts of strategy and leverage that we address in this section of this book. If you deviate from these concepts (and people always want to deviate) your divorce is more likely to be botched, along with your family, finances, and future.

ASHLEY & CHRISTOPHER BRUCE
CONTROL YOUR DIFFICULT DIVORCE

We note that later in this book, in the sections titled *Move Forward & Avoid Distractions* and *Resolution Focused Litigation*, we expand upon the basic concepts of leverage and strategy discussed in this chapter and explain how to handle divorce litigation, your spouse, and others in a manner that gives you the best likelihood of obtaining a fair divorce settlement as soon as possible while minimizing collateral damage to your family. However, you need to understand the basics of divorce leverage and strategy covered in this chapter before you move on to these sections.

As a word of warning, the *Best Divorce* strategies and concepts we'll be explaining are not always engineered for enjoyment. Your reaction to some of what follows might be to feel uncomfortable. However, having the *Best Divorce* is probably going to require you to step outside of your comfort zone and act differently, because how you've acted leading up to now was a big contribution to the problem we are trying to solve. Nothing we advocate is immoral or illegal. Everything we're going to tell you is designed to make your life better as soon as possible, and in the long term, make your family and finances far better off than they would otherwise be. Isn't that what you want?

To quote my (Chris') father, "If you keep doing what you've always done, you'll get what you've always got." If you want to make things better than they are now, then realize that "you have to change to change." Keep reading *Section #2: Learn the Basics of Leverage & Strategy* and we'll tell you how.

How People Make Decisions in a Complex Divorce

I (Chris) have an accounting degree. When I was in college, my passion was tax accounting and not much else (which probably explains why I didn't have much of a social life back then). In any event, at some point as part of getting my number-crunching diploma, I begrudgingly had to satisfy some college dean's vision of a well-rounded education and take a few elective classes outside the business school.

I don't remember much now about these classes besides how the students at the University of Florida's liberal arts college seemed more outgoing (or less nerdy) than those in the accounting school, but that does not help you much right now. If I had any idea at the time that I was going to break up marriages for a living as a divorce lawyer, I would have probably paid more attention to the professors. Especially, if they were lecturing about the Abraham Maslow and his famous "Hierarchy of Needs."

So, what does one of the first supposedly famous American born psychologist's seemingly esoteric hypothesis on human needs have to do with your divorce? Everything. Understanding why people make decisions in a complex divorce is crucial to the development of your *Best Divorce* strategy. This is because if you know *why* people make decisions in divorce, you can develop a plan to help them choose to make decisions that result in your desired outcome.

Fortunately, once boiled down, the reason why people make decisions in divorce is not any different than how people approach any other type of decision-making. People always make decisions for a reason, even if the reason is subconscious. And this is where Abraham Maslow's "Hierarchy of Needs" becomes important. Maslow's theorem is pretty much spot on to what drives most all divorce decision-making.

According to Maslow (1943), all people are motivated to achieve certain needs, in an order of priority. Once lower level, basic needs are satisfied, people advance to satisfying higher level needs. Also, the longer that a person's lower level needs go unmet, the stronger the desire becomes to meet the need. Maslow's original five-stage hierarchy of needs hypothesis is that people are motivated to satisfying their needs in the following order (courtesy of **www.simplypsychology.org**):

1. **_Biological and Psychological Needs_**: *air, food, shelter, warmth, sex and sleep;*

2. **<u>Safety Needs</u>**: *protection from the elements, security, order, law, stability, and freedom from fear;*
3. **<u>Love and Belongingness Needs</u>**: *friendship, intimacy, affection, and love;*
4. **<u>Esteem Needs</u>**: *achievement, mastery, independence, status, dominance, prestige, self-respect, respect from others;*
5. **<u>Self-Actualization Needs</u>**: *realizing personal potential, self-fulfillment, seeking personal growth and peak experiences.*

So, how does this all relate to your divorce? Maslow's "Needs Hierarchy" explains what will motivate your spouse's decision-making during your divorce. Your spouse's first instinct will be to make sure their biological, psychological and safety needs are met. This translates into making decisions out of need to pay their bills, having a place to live, and feeling safe. If these needs are not initially being met, or if there is a fear they will not be met, then your spouse's behavior and actions during the divorce and in settlement negotiations will be to provide for and preserve these needs as soon as possible. Knowing this allows you to develop a *Best Divorce* strategy that takes into account your spouse's anticipated motivations and behaviors.

Once the basic needs are taken care of, then your spouse will be motivated by what Maslow calls the love and belongingness needs and esteem needs. What this translates into is that if your spouse knows there is going to be enough money to go around, then what is going to motivate them in their divorce decisions will be driven by (1) their desire to preserve relationships with other people (sometimes you, if they don't want the divorce, but always their relationships with friends and family) and (2) their desire to preserve their reputation to others (this is especially true if your spouse is a narcissist or egomaniac).

As you might suspect, if you can understand or predict what relationships your spouse wants to preserve, and become knowledgeable about any of their potential or perceived reputation issues, you will work this understanding into your *Best Divorce* strategy.

We'll state things differently for those who read through the above and were turned off or confused by all the Abraham Maslow "psycho-babble." What you need to know is that people are programmed to make decisions based on their perceived needs. Generally, as more money is added to the equation, your spouse's focus of what they want out of the divorce will graduate from basic economic priorities to preserving family relationships and then

their social status.

The bottom line is if you understand what your spouse's needs will be, then you can probably predict most of how they will behave during the divorce and what they will want out of the divorce. You can then leverage this understanding to develop a divorce strategy around your spouse's anticipated motivations to give yourself the best odds of obtaining an efficient, quick settlement and preventing your divorce case from going "off track." This is possibly worth more economically to you than anything else related to your divorce, so take the time to find out what will motivate your spouse's decision-making.

ASHLEY & CHRISTOPHER BRUCE
CONTROL YOUR DIFFICULT DIVORCE

The First Mover Advantage
(Move First, Unannounced, and Don't Back Off)

There is a "first mover advantage" with divorce. Given the tremendous personal and strategic preparation required by the *Best Divorce*, your spouse will be at an extreme disadvantage if the divorce begins with you already having "your act together" (see *Section #1*) and executing on a well thought out divorce strategy. If you move first, unannounced, and don't back off, your spouse will feel like they have their back up against a wall and that everything they are doing is "reactive" to you as they try to keep their head above water.

Psychologically, this can be a huge driver to an early settlement. For whatever reason, in our law practice, this seems especially true with women, or when the unprepared spouse feels like they are too busy with their business or occupation to defend themselves in their divorce.

To be clear, we're not advocating that you do anything illegal or immoral. That is never acceptable. You need to be professional and humane in all of your divorce dealings or you will suffer in the long run. Our point is you need to be first. Second place is an honorable recognition in the Olympics but in divorce it could mean you lose big.

Prepare yourself mentally for the divorce and then move forward before making your intended actions obvious to your spouse. It is a highly effective strategy to make your spouse feel like they "have no choice" than to settle because you've been "plotting the divorce for forever" and that you've "thought of everything." When this happens, you increase the likelihood that your divorce resolves quickly on fair terms, and everyone is better in the long term.

Moving first is almost required if you are in a long-term abusive relationship or your spouse controls the finances (which usually only happens when there is a relationship imbalance). If your spouse has trained you through years of mistreatment to be their submissive "door mat," then they are going to wake up each day believing they can continue to walk all over you. In these relationships, the person in your spouse's position rarely anticipates you standing up for yourself and filing for divorce. As a result, when you file for divorce, they are likely to be caught off guard, and do not have time to move money or manipulate their finances. Catching your spouse with their "pants down" before they have had time to do "divorce planning" will drastically limit the ways your divorce can get sidetracked.

Just as important as moving first is not backing off once you set your *Best Divorce* strategy into motion. There is no point in following our advice to do everything necessary to prepare for divorce and develop your *Best Divorce* strategy, if you stall implementation of the strategy shortly after your spouse is alerted to the divorce. When this happens, you open yourself up to numerous ways for your divorce to become more involved than it needs to be. Face the music: your spouse might not be happy with the divorce and could be motivated to manipulate money and people. Why should you extend an already difficult process while giving your spouse the opportunity to add further delays, costs, and cause collateral damage?

Many people tell us they don't want to file for divorce first because they believe it will look better to their friends and family if they are instead, the person responding to the divorce lawsuit. We believe this approach is ignorant and short-sighted. As a practical matter, any "ill will" friends and family might have for you for initiating the divorce, will be outweighed by the divorce being over sooner. The longer you delay, the more opportunities will come up which can cause conflict between you, your spouse, and loved ones.

ASHLEY & CHRISTOPHER BRUCE
CONTROL YOUR DIFFICULT DIVORCE

It is far better for your family, and you in the long term, if your
divorce is settled quickly, then to go through a protracted, nasty divorce that eradicates your finances, family and friends. The latter result is far less likely to happen if you develop a *Best Divorce* strategy and are the first to move forward without backing off.

Believe it or not, in many instances, friends and family could see your divorce coming for years. They might even be relieved the divorce is actually happening because they know deep down, it is what you need (this is especially true with children who are young adults). Further, odds are that if your spouse is going to complain to your family about you filing for divorce first, then one of two things are likely true: (1) they likely would complain to your family about you no matter what happened in the divorce, even if they filed first or (2) they would never file for divorce and you'd forever be stuck in limbo, living the life you are reading this book to improve.

Although this book is not a state-specific legal treatise, for a moment, we'll address whether there is a legal benefit to being the first to file for divorce. We believe there is, but only if your case involves complex legal, financial, or child custody issues. We say this because, while most divorce cases never go to trial, the odds of trial are substantially higher when there are complex legal issues, a business or substantial assets to value, or difficult child custody issues. If your case has complicating factors that has higher odds of judicial intervention than it is in your best interest to control the presentation to the judge as much as possible.

If you are the first to the courthouse in Florida where we practice and in most other jurisdictions you are better able to control the trial because your lawyer will be the first to present in opening statements and closing arguments, and you will have the chance to present your witnesses first, with the opportunity to present witnesses to rebut your spouse's witnesses. With a great judge, the order of presentation makes no difference, but sometimes the psychological impact of your legal team making the first and final points for the judge to remember makes it easier to decide "close call" issues in your favor. When there is a lot at stake, you want to control as much as you can and make it as easy as possible for the judge to rule for you. Filing first allows you one more way to do this.

Do Not Create Short Term Cash Flow Problems

The easiest way to have a miserable divorce is caused by giving away significant financial leverage to the other spouse before the divorce even gets going. Although creating this problem is unbelievably easy, the fix usually requires a lot of time and money for any divorce lawyer to fix. If you throw away financial leverage early, in many cases, you'll have to take a less than desirable settlement because the litigation costs of correcting the mess you enabled will not be worth it. Does this sound like fun to you? We bet not.

The way to avoid the above-described, self-inflicted divorce hell is to stay away from making decisions that will create short term cash flow problems for you during your divorce. Regardless of whether you control more assets or income than your spouse, if you are not in control of your cash flow, you will be fighting an uphill battle from the beginning. Believe us when we tell you that you never want to be fighting an uphill battle in your divorce- unless you are someone who enjoys protracted and expensive misery.

ASHLEY & CHRISTOPHER BRUCE
CONTROL YOUR DIFFICULT DIVORCE

We especially advise our female clients who depend on their husbands for support to never make decisions prior to an anticipated divorce that put them in a short-term cash flow crunch. For whatever reason, at least in our experience, the first instinct of many women is to make short term financial stability their highest priority. While this is a great quality during their marriage (and in life), it is a huge problem in their divorce when their ill-intentioned husband preys upon them by cutting off financial support.

When this happens, it is very difficult for many women to emotionally handle the short-term cash flow crunch. As a result, some end up accepting what is otherwise a disgusting, one-sided, settlement favoring their husband just so they don't have to deal with anymore financial pressure. This can happen just as easily to men when their wives control most of the assets, and they do not earn enough to support themselves and their children independently.

Cash flow problems during divorce are equally devastating if you are the spouse who has the higher income or control of the assets. If you do not control your cash flow, your decision-making during your divorce is going to be clouded by watching your money evaporate at the hands of your less wealthy spouse. Even if you have the ability to tap assets to ride out the divorce, it is going to be financially and emotionally expensive. Many people in this position will accept undesirable settlements to "stop the bleeding" as they cannot stand the thought of their life's savings or family fortune being eroded. This is a shame for many reasons, especially as the result likely could have been avoided with proper divorce planning.

The most common way people create a short-term cash flow problem is by moving out of the marital home. For the economically dependent spouse, moving out of the house and creating a new set of housing expenses in the form of a rental or lease payment makes them dependent on their spouse to pay their newly created expenses. This is not a good place to be when you are negotiating for your financial future, especially if you anticipate your spouse being upset with the divorce. The absolute last thing you'll need to worry about as you negotiate your financial future is paying new, current expenses.

While it is true that your lawyer may be able to eventually force your spouse to pay for your expenses through the courts, it usually takes several months to get this to happen if you go through the court system. Many people end up entering into absurd settlements to qualm the perceived belief that they will be "starving" financially for several months. Although this may sound ridiculous to read, it happens. And the problem is one of perception. Multi-millionaires enter into bad divorce settlements all the time out of their perceived fear that they will not be able to maintain their standard of living.

Leaving the marital home can be equally problematic if you are the higher wage earner. In our practice, we continue to be amazed at the propensity for people to expand their housing expenses to fit their income. As extreme as it sounds, there are people who are earning upwards of seven figures a year that would be crippled financially if they had a second housing payment, especially if their ability to earn a high income is dependent upon them maintaining a high credit rating.

If most of your income goes towards paying the mortgage before you move out, most of your income is going to continue being used to pay your mortgage after you move out if you have to maintain your credit. If this is you, then you will be creating the situation where you will need to deplete your assets to pay your new housing expenses while you most of your income goes towards paying for your spouse to live in the home you moved out of.

And good luck thinking that you'll just move out and stop paying the mortgage. Most judges will "preserve the status quo" on a temporary basis. This means that if you move out after historically paying the mortgage, your judge will probably keep you out of the house and make you keep paying the mortgage. At this point, you either go to jail for not doing what the judge orders you to do, or you continue to allow your spouse to hold the financial leverage in the divorce.

In either case, you will be operating at an extreme disadvantage. Also, you've likely aggravated the one person wearing a black robe who will be determining the result in your case, and earned the honor of being labeled a "deadbeat" by the other lawyer each time there is a court hearing. None of this is good news. All of this should be avoided.

Thankfully, besides dealing with being a bit uncomfortable in the short term, it is usually easy to avoid the creation of short term cash flow problems if you take the time to plan out a *Best Divorce* strategy. In many instances, all you need to do is be the person who remains in the marital home. It can be uncomfortable in the short term to be under the same roof with your spouse as you navigate your divorce, but this is worth it if you avoid being on the bad end of a cash flow crunch.

If anyone has to move out, let it be your spouse. If domestic violence or extreme emotional abuse is an issue, then speak to your lawyer, as there are options on how to handle this. You should never stay in a situation where you believe you or your children are in danger of physical harm from your spouse, without taking action. Sometimes, it is possible to obtain court orders requiring your spouse to live outside of the home. Otherwise, if you stay in the house and avoid becoming cash flow poor, you will side-step one of the easiest ways people turn their divorce into a disaster.

Be the One to Control the Money & Documents

We originally wrote this chapter in the wake of another mass shooting in the United States. The shooting gained particular notoriety not just for the horrific execution style killings, but for the way President Obama politicized his gun control agenda immediately after the shootings. The President's basic premise was that if there are tougher gun laws, then domestic terrorists will not be able to do horrific things with guns.

Conceptually speaking, President Obama made a logical point. If you keep terrorists away from weapons of mass destruction, then it is harder for terrorists to cause mass destruction. As a practical matter, with gun control, the issue is complicated because terrorists are not always naturally inclined to following the law and, the fact is, no matter what law is enacted, there are already hundreds of millions of firearms in the United States (several of which are in our possession). Unfortunately, it seems unlikely any law will ever take these firearms off the black markets that many terrorists and other criminals frequent.

Fortunately, "divorce terrorists" are easier to control than most other terrorists. "Divorce terrorists?" "Who are they?" you might be wondering. "Divorce terrorists" are the spouses who behave in a manner that makes your divorce an expensive, exhausting, and a living hell.

"Divorce terrorists" can take many forms. They can be a jilted spouse intent on ruining your life for leaving the marriage, just as easily as they can be the controlling, narcissistic/sociopathic bastard type of person who tries to manipulate you through mind games and intimidation tactics. What could be worse? How about the fact that these "divorce terrorists" use your money to fuel their mayhem?

Fortunately, it does not take a Harvard educated policy analyst to stop "divorce terrorists." A great deal of their harm can be cut off before it begins by cutting off their access to money. How do you do this? Simple. Be the one to control the money in your divorce. This is usually easy. Be the one to go to the bank and move most of your money into accounts you control, before your spouse does. If you don't have access to their account, speak to your lawyer. There are likely options in your jurisdiction for putting at least a temporary freeze on the main financial accounts early on. For now, all you need to know is that you can eradicate divorce terrorists when you control the money.

ASHLEY & CHRISTOPHER BRUCE
CONTROL YOUR DIFFICULT DIVORCE

You are asking for trouble if you hesitate and give your spouse the chance to do bad things like cutting off your cash flow or making your money "disappear." Yes, there are processes your lawyer can utilize to restore cash flow and find the money, but do you really want to go through all of that? The *Best Divorce* you deserve is all about controlling the divorce process and getting it over as soon as possible without that type of preventable stress.

The bottom line is that if you control the money, you eliminate many of the problems that unnecessarily complicate divorce while creating a much higher likelihood of getting your spouse to the bargaining table quickly and settling on fair terms. This is the one of the main goals of the *Best Divorce*, and should be one of your main goals too, unless you have an ulterior motive that involves charity work involving transfers of wealth to divorce lawyers like me.

Just as important as controlling the money is getting early access to information. This is especially important if your spouse has been up to no good or you are "in the dark" on the marital finances. Odds are, you know where the information is that allows you to be more informed. If you don't know, people can help you figure it out. Further, when your spouse believes you "have everything," there may be an extra incentive on their part to settle, even if this motivation is ultimately unjustified. Obtain and at least copy all of this information now, before there is any mention of divorce.

The mechanics of this are explained in granular, step by step detail in the Bruce Law Firm's Book, The Women's Guide to Getting Organized for Divorce. This book is available for free download at www.GetOrganizedForDivorce.com. Although the book is tailored towards women considering divorce from a narcissistic or emotionally abusive/manipulative husband, the content is extremely useful to both men and women alike.

For now, just know it is critical to obtain access to your spouse's transgressions and marital finances before anything goes forward with divorce unless you believe your safety is at risk. Once there is mention of divorce, you should count on this information being moved, harder to find than it is now, and sanitized once it is located. You can help significantly reduce legal fees and speed up the divorce process by obtaining the key information about your spouse and finances before anything is put into motion.

If you are nervous about controlling the money or gathering information, remember that it is likely that half the money is yours and you are doing nothing wrong by using legal means to gather information about your marital and financial situation. The latter parts of this book and an ethical and competent lawyer will help you deal with coordinating the logistics and legality of all of this.

Don't be one of the people that comes up with endless excuses about why you should not or cannot control the money or have full access to information. These excuses are copouts. If you find yourself thinking this way then, with all due respect, you are not prepared for the *Best Divorce*. Before you do anything else, you need to re-read *Section 1: Get Your Act Together*; and go see a qualified therapist to help you break out of your likely co-dependent tenancies that will put you at an extreme disadvantage in your divorce (and life after the divorce) if left unaddressed.

Being a Nice-Guy or Gal Will Not Get Your Family Back

The mind is a powerful thing. It is also dangerous. Especially, for those who are depressed about their spouse pursing a divorce over their objection. Many of these people go through an initial period of depression and deny the fact that their spouse wants to pursue a life apart from them. If you are one of these people, you need to understand that you are not going to get your spouse back by entering into an overly generous settlement agreement. Being the "nice-guy" or "nice gal" will not get your family back and can make it harder for you to have any semblance of economic stability in your future life and relationships. Instead, you need to find a good therapist to understand the reality of your situation and develop a plan for recovering from the end of your relationship.

In our experience, for whatever reason, men who have had an affair and codependent women are more prone to entering into financially crippling settlement agreements for the purpose of trying to win their spouse back or get them to change. They do this with the thought that giving their spouse everything they ask for in the divorce, will help their spouse understand their unconditional love and devotion to the relationship and either forgive them for the affair, or in the case of abusive relationships, stop being abusive. They think that by being the "nice guy/gal" and "the giver," their spouse will "wake up" and realize how much they love them, and they'll get back the relationship they lost. In making what we call these "nice guy agreements," the "nice guy" spouse often over-extends themselves financially, creating an unrealistic burden for them to meet (or not enough money to live on) going forward.

The good part about these "nice guy agreements" is they get the divorce over relatively quickly. That is where the advantages end. The problems with these agreements primarily surface later, when the "nice guy spouse" realizes the relationship is really over, their spouse isn't coming back, and that their life is miserable because they gave away nearly all of their money and made unrealistic promises (like a high alimony obligation) they cannot keep.

Unfortunately, for most of these people, there is rarely any real legal recourse. Most divorce laws encourage finality in settlement agreements. It is usually impossible to change a property settlement, and many judges will not change an outrageously unfair agreed-upon alimony obligation, unless there is a drastic change in financial circumstances. The argument that you woke up a year after your divorce to the reality that you made a bad deal while in a state of depression/desperation is likely not going to get you anywhere.

If you are a "nice guy" (or nice gal) whose spouse is seeking a divorce, odds are that you've never understood your spouse's "love language." As explained in Dr. Gary Chapman's book, *"The Five Love Languages,"* spouses usually feel love from their spouse in different ways. Some people feel loved when their spouse provides financially for them. Others feel loved when their spouse spends time with them, or touches them, or does chores for them, etc. Relationship problems arise when spouses do not understand each other's love languages for long periods of time. This leads to spouses drifting apart, and in some cases, seeking divorce.

You should read *"The Five Love Languages"* to understand this in more depth. The bottom line that you need to understand is that if your spouse's reaction to your years of hard work to provide for the family is a divorce petition, you are not going to win your spouse back by bending over backwards further, to give your spouse more financial support. This is because your spouse is likely leaving you because their "love language" does not involve money, and you have not understood their real "love language" for a long period of time, which your spouse equates with you being incapable of meeting their needs in a relationship.

Similarly, if you are in an abusive relationship, such as one involving a narcissistic or manipulative spouse, you need to realize that agreeing to a generous settlement is not going to get your spouse to change. In our experience, abusers and narcissists are like leaches. They just suck the life out of people. These people never change and will likely only view your generosity as a sign of weakness.

The point to all of this is that offering up a generous financial settlement is not going to convince your spouse to come back to you if the reason they are leaving does not relate to your inability to provide financial support. Although your spouse probably appreciates your financial support, they are likely divorcing you because you never spoke their real "love language," and not because of a lack of money. When this is the case, giving your spouse more money than they deserve in a divorce settlement will not save your marriage, and will only serve to make life harder for you in the future. If your goal is to save your marriage, then you need to understand why your spouse feels their needs were unmet, and then find a way to meet those needs. Sadly, this is sometimes not possible, especially in long term marriages where one spouse has come to the decision that their spouse will "never change."

You need to get to a good therapist immediately if you believe that any of this chapter describes your situation. The money you spend on a good therapist is far less than the long-term costs of entering into a one-sided financial settlement agreement. See ww.StayMarriedFlorida.com for a few great recommendations for therapists in the Florida area. If you are resistant to therapy, then at least remember that a *Best Divorce* strategy never involves entering into unfair or unrealistic settlement agreements. Doing so is not going to save your marriage, and will cost you more in the long term, than paying for a lawyer to get you a fair deal.

Guilty Conscience Agreements & Exposing Their Secrets

Everyone has a secret they don't want other people to know about. Do you? More importantly, does your spouse? In many instances, these "secrets", which can range from adultery to corporate espionage or fraud, can all end up being exposed through a competent divorce lawyer conducting "discovery" in your divorce case. Your understanding of these "secrets," and the value your spouse attaches to them, can be the difference between quickly negotiating a fair settlement and several years of miserable and costly divorce litigation. Leveraging "secrets" through "guilty conscience agreements" could be your quick path to the *Best Divorce*.

One of the stereotypical "secrets" is adultery. Is your spouse secretly spending nights away from the family to sleep with someone else? Oftentimes when this happens, the person having the affair feels guilty about what they are doing. An affair that started with one little lie has turned into a life of lies. Imagine always having to lie to your spouse, children, and coworkers about seemingly everything in order to create excuses to sneak off with your paramour. This isn't much different for other lies, corporate betrayals, and silent secrets that compound for the worse with the passage of time. For normal people, over time, they feel like their life is one big, huge lie, and they dread the day that they are exposed for betraying or embarrassing their family, business partners, or employers. When long-term "secrets" are exposed, reputations are ruined. At least, that is the perception the person holding down the "secret" sometimes feels.

So, what does all of this have to do with your divorce? If you obtain undeniable proof of your spouse's inappropriate conduct, and strategically convey, or offer to convey, said proof, your case can be over fast. Your spouse, who may have been dreading the day they are found out, now knows "you know," and dreads what you may do with the information. If timed correctly (and timing is everything here), your spouse's realization their secret may not be safe can be the "nail in the coffin" of finishing up a fair and reasonable settlement negotiation.

If your spouse is on the borderline of accepting your settlement offer at the time they are hit with the reality that their "secrets" will be exposed and dissected in the divorce, the odds go up that they stop messing around and settle the case on fair terms before further transgression. At this point, your divorce is done, and there is no need further elaborate on your spouse's improper conduct. You get a fair deal and your soon to be former spouse can go back to keeping their secrets. Life goes on.

The strategy with turning "secrets" into settlements depends on two things: timing and proof. Of these, timing is the most important. "Secrets" tend to slip away when you tip off your spouse about what you know before you gather proof. Likewise, if you tell your spouse you know their "secrets" before developing your *Best Divorce* legal strategy, you will likely fail to optimize the ability to incentivize settlement. There is not a hard and fast rule to timing communicating your knowledge of your spouse's "secrets" during the litigation and negotiation process. This matter is something you need to discuss with your lawyer early on so that it is incorporated into a larger solution-focused case strategy.

In some instances, your lawyer may need to take action to "infer knowledge of something," without "putting all the cards on the table." In other instances, the best route is as simple as showing a private investigator's video or report during mediation, if settlement talks start to break down. Other times, the "secret" needs to be tested during the litigation and only brought out in court to show your spouse's lack of credibility. There are countless other ways to bring out "secrets" and the bottom-line *Best Divorce* strategy if you believe your spouse has a "secret" is to discuss it first with a lawyer before telling your spouse. Telling your spouse early on limits leverage and is not going to save your marriage (your marriage is not going to last or be anything special if you attempt intimidating your spouse into staying with you).

As far as proof of "secrets," you need to make the proof undeniable. If you have to give documentation, you want to make it clear to your spouse that "they are nailed." As an example, if your spouse is having an affair, then have a private investigator create indisputable documentation, preferably on video, preferably of multiple instances. Combine this with evidence of "the story" your spouse told you, your children, or their colleagues about his whereabouts or activities on some of the occasions they were being unfaithful. Evidence your spouse was with their paramour when they were supposed to be at birthday party, graduation, or corporate closing has a way of being "influential."

ASHLEY & CHRISTOPHER BRUCE
CONTROL YOUR DIFFICULT DIVORCE

The same concept goes for any other type of "secret." If your spouse is messing around with corporate betrayals, then your legal team needs to get the documents and, if possible, witness statements to prove the misdeeds before anything else happens.

The goal with proof is to gather enough information to show your spouse there is no way on earth they'll be able to put a different spin on the facts. Sometimes, gathering this proof costs some money upfront, but is worth it in the long term, to your finances and family if your case resolves quickly.

So, you might be wondering, is this "extortion"? Can you go to jail for leveraging your spouse's "secrets" to get your divorce over quickly, and spare your family and finances the strain or protracted divorce litigation? The bottom line is you need to talk to your lawyer who is familiar with the laws of your jurisdiction. But in our opinion, the answer is "absolutely not" if your case is settled based on you and your spouse determining if it is mutually beneficial to end your case on fair terms, without engaging in further discovery and exploration of issues that would be relevant to your divorce case. We are absolutely not advising you to engage in the equivalent of threatening to ruin your spouse's life if they do not agree to an extremely one-sided settlement that they'd never obtain through the laws of any court. That is extortion, and we will have no part in it, and neither should you.

Our point is that, engaging in the process required to properly prepare your divorce case for trial can make your spouse uncomfortable, if the process is going to naturally uncover facts they'd prefer to keep hidden. You are not "extorting" your spouse by having your lawyer engage in the normal due diligence necessary to obtain the relief you are entitled to seek in divorce court. The fact that your spouse might not like the facts uncovered during the litigation process is their problem, not yours. If your spouse agrees to a fair and reasonable settlement to avoid the costs of experiencing your legal team engaging in legally permissible trial preparation, then that is their choice and it's probably a wise one.

There are many ways to obtain the *Best Divorce* and realizing and documenting your spouse's "secrets" can be one of them. If there are "secrets" in your relationship, you need to have them well documented. Further, if it becomes necessary to disclose these "secrets," the timing needs to be carefully calculated. Finally, although it probably seems "self-serving" for a lawyer to write in their book to "consult a lawyer" on an issue, this is one of the areas where you need to make sure your actions are within the boundaries of what is legal. For this reason, you should consult with a lawyer before implementing the strategies outlined in this section. (On this note, we note that the Bruce Law Firm has a book on how to find, hire, and work with your divorce lawyer that is available for free download at www.AllAboutDivorceLawyers.com).

Bringing Their Extra-Marital Relationships to Light (and Keeping Yours in the Dark)

It is no mystery that many divorce filings come about when someone discovers their spouse is involved in a relationship with another person. With this being the case, you'd think by now that it would be common knowledge how to deal with adultery in a divorce. However, this chapter is being written after observing countless highly educated people botch integration of infidelity into their larger divorce strategy. While nearly all jurisdictions have "no fault" laws that allow a divorce without proving adultery, the fact is that your infidelity or your spouse's infidelity can be the difference between you obtaining a fair settlement quickly or enduring a divorce war.

The misunderstanding we see time and time again concerning adultery is the attitude of "my state is a no fault state so my spouse's affair (or my affair) is not relevant to the divorce." Correction: affairs are relevant! If you do not understand this, you will either (1) miss the opportunity to use your spouse's affair as leverage to help end your divorce case or (2) overly complicate your divorce case (and irreparably harm the relationship with your spouse) by flaunting your own adultery or new relationship before the divorce is finalized.

Although it may be hard to believe, people who are not serial adulterers often cringe at the thought of their spouse finding out about their affair. Although the "cheating spouse" may not want to stay married, they feel terrible about the relationship ending because of the affair. Further, and perhaps most importantly, the cheating spouse is usually very embarrassed about the affair and would rather have friends and family believe they met their paramour after their divorce. In other cases, the spouse has no remorse for the affair, but out of desperation to maintain the relationship with their new partner (who could be the first person they've loved in years) they will do anything they can to keep their paramour from being involved in their divorce case (especially when the paramour is also cheating on their partner).

For this reason, it is not uncommon for people who have been having an affair to desire a quick settlement to their divorce. This is especially the case with women who have been having an affair. The important thing to remember about affairs is that your divorce case can be over quickly if your litigation strategy makes clear that (1) you have knowledge of your spouse's affair and (2) you are going to investigate and expose the details of the affair, and question the paramour, if the divorce case is not settled quickly on fair terms. If your marriage is over, then the affair, and details of it, can be highly influential to ending your divorce quickly.

Although the exact strategy implemented will need to be specific to your situation, you cannot forget that affairs are relevant, and you should not fail to consider incorporating your spouse's affair into your *Best Divorce* strategy. Don't be one of those people who buries their head in the sand and ignores the affair in their divorce. Although it seems painful to pursue information about an affair, most of the work can be done by your lawyer and paid professionals, without your involvement, and you never have to know the exact details of the infidelity.

Further, long term, your current pain and feelings of sadness over the affair can be far outweighed by the feeling of anger you may have, if you realize you left dollars on the table in your settlement, or allowed your spouse to railroad you in the divorce by not confronting the affair correctly.

Equally important as confronting a spouse's affair, is keeping your infidelity or new relationship out of sight. Your spouse's discovery that you are in a new relationship will in no way help your divorce case and will almost always complicate your divorce. This is true even when your spouse is the one who first had the affair, and your new relationship only started after the divorce case started.

Come on now, did you really think your spouse would, during your divorce, be thrilled to "congratulate" you for moving on from them? Well, they will not. They usually are infuriated. Even if they have "no right" to be. People who are angry usually do not settle their divorce cases quickly. This is not good for your bank account. Don't do it. The bottom line on this issue, if it applies to you, is do not flaunt your new relationship and try to keep it out of sight. It doesn't matter whether you feel you are morally justified in the new relationship based on mistreatment during the marriage, your spouse having an affair, your spouse filing for divorce, or anything else. If you want your divorce over, on fair terms, as soon as possible, try to keep your new relationship "under wraps." Better yet, put new relationships on hold until the divorce is over.

And one more word on affairs. Any experienced divorce lawyer or therapist will tell you that as long as your spouse is not a serial adulterer or inflicted with a personality disorder, the discovery of the affair can actually be an opportunity to improve your marriage. Oftentimes, the affair is an outward symptom of a relationship between two people who are not fulfilling each other's needs who, over a long period of time, simply drifted apart from each other.

Although you are reading a chapter on divorce strategy, you should remember that an affair does not have to be the end of your marriage. If you and your spouse are committed to improving your relationship, and all ties with the paramour are eliminated, the affair can actually be the impetus for an overwhelmingly positive relationship transformation. We know this may sound ridiculous, but it is true. You should consider consulting an experienced couple's therapist to discuss the options for dealing with an affair that do not involve divorce. At risk of being repetitive, if you do not know a therapist, we've listed plenty of the great ones in South Florida at www.StayMarriedFlorida.com.

Top Five Other "Should Be Obvious" Mistakes to Avoid

The portions of the book dedicated to learning the basics of leverage and strategy cover mostly the non-obvious, or counter-intuitive aspects of *Best Divorce* strategies we implement in our law practice. So far, we have left out most of what would qualify as "obviously, you should do not do this" type advice. However, we're including a top five list of "should be obvious" mistakes to avoid in this chapter because we are amazed with the propensity for highly educated people to make these mistakes and complicate their divorce. The bottom line is, do not make any of the mistakes below and you have a much higher likelihood of having the *Best Divorce* possible.

Should be Obvious Mistake #1:

Do not underestimate your spouse. You married them and few people know you better than they do. Most of the time, they are smarter than you think. They might not have taken any recent interest in anything that involves you. However, odds are that most people who were of the quality to marry anyone who takes the time to read this book are going to be the types of spouses who will "wake up" and pay serious attention to everything in a divorce. They are the type of spouse who may never have read a bank statement or general ledger, but will devote days, even weeks, to studying yours or developing their own *Best Divorce* strategy -- if it means more money or retribution. Never lose sight of this. Never underestimate your spouse.

Should be Obvious Mistake #2:

Do not share your *Best Divorce* strategy or the fact you are considering divorce with anyone who does not have a legal duty to keep your plans a secret. Preferably, keep your strategy between you, your lawyer, and your personal therapist only. This means you should never discuss your divorce strategy or plans with your friends or your family, especially your spouse's friends and family. In case you need an explanation, the reasons for doing this are: (1) if you end up changing your mind and deciding to save the marriage (as many people, including you, may possibly do) then nobody know the difference, or will attempt to talk you out of this very personal decision, or remind you of this painful time later; (2) people are terrible at keeping secrets, which means news of your divorce and strategy will spread, and what may have been your only strategy for efficiently resolving your divorce would be ruined; (3) some of your friends will be uncomfortable or at least want to avoid you, if they are subjected to talk of divorce or wanting a divorce; (4) business or investment partners will find a way to disassociate themselves and stay away from you until the divorce is finalized and for a while thereafter (they don't want their money or their own secrets exposed or tied up in your divorce), and if you save your marriage, they will unfairly assume they still need to avoid you; and (5) your spouse's friends and family will never understand where you are coming from, and will use whatever you tell them to help your spouse, sometimes even convincing them of baseless fears.

Should be Obvious Mistake #3:

Understand that bank accounts always leave traces, but cash is harder to trace. If your financial records will show you doing something nefarious, idiotic, or classless, you need to count on it being brought out in a divorce. As stated above, your spouse probably knows you better than anyone, and will therefore know what to look for in your financial records and be motivated to study every piece of information they get their hands on. If they do not, then you can probably count on their paid professionals having the motivation. Do not be lulled into thinking your spouse or their lawyer will not look at your financial records. They will. And probably more than anyone ever has before.

Should be Obvious Mistake #4:

Do not make a settlement offer to your spouse until you know what is fair and reasonable for your situation. Consult with an attorney before you offer anything to your spouse. What you will pay for several hours of competent legal advice is miniscule when compared to the cost of your spouse being angry about your reneging on giving them what you promised in a divorce settlement. For whatever reason, this is especially the case with women whose husbands are the breadwinner. If you are the breadwinner spouse, do not promise details of how you will support your spouse after the marriage until (1) you determine from a lawyer what is legally required and (2) you have studied your finances enough to determine the amount of money you are actually capable of paying to your spouse after taking care of your reasonable expenses after the divorce.

Should be Obvious Mistake #5:

Understand that if you put it in writing or do it on the internet, someone is going to see it or find it, save what you do, and use it against you later. Assume any email or text message you send to your spouse or their family and friends will be downloaded into a database, and then searched for key word phrases having to do with your divorce. If you assume that a judge with "discretion" to determine your financial future will read every written communication that could be related to your divorce, then you will probably put less in writing. Also, as ridiculous as it sounds, there are numerous people in the baby boomer generation that have completely botched their divorce strategy by posting or being active on Facebook, other social media outlets, or blogs. Do not be one of these people if your internet persona is opposite to your *Best Divorce* strategy.

If you remember anything, avoid breaking the five items of "should be obvious" divorce advice listed above. If you can do this, which is not always easy, you will allow yourself the best odds of obtaining the *Best Divorce* possible

Section 3: Finalize Your Best Divorce & Best Life Strategies

Best Divorce & Best Life Strategy Overview

All of the book up through now has been dedicated to getting you prepared to utilize the divorce process to move on from your marriage and ultimately improve your life. Doing this properly requires a great deal of soul searching, some learning, and a lot of preparation. At this point, you have done most of the legwork involved with having the *Best Divorce* possible. You are just about at the proverbial "starting line" of what will hopefully be a divorce that is resolved on fair terms as soon as possible. All you need to do now is refine your plan for moving forward with your divorce, and your life after your divorce, so that you can put that plan into action.

Throughout this book, we've referred to the development of your *Best Divorce* strategy and your *Best Life* strategy. These strategies represent your "plan" for what happens in the divorce and in your life after the divorce. Although everything you have done to this point is important, the preparation of a proper *Best Divorce* strategy and *Best Life* strategy is the most important thing you can do to ensure that your divorce and your life after the divorce is the best that it can be.

This section of the book takes you through what you need to do to finalize your *Best Divorce* and *Best Life* strategies with your lawyer and therapist. You'll need to start by refining your goals to what is realistic, and then coming up with an "action plan" that makes those goals a reality. As you go through this process there are several important things you need to keep in mind and include in your *Best Divorce* and *Best Life* strategies, and in the following chapters, we'll take you through what you need to know.

Work with Your Lawyer & Therapist to Refine Your Goals

The primary driver of your *Best Divorce* strategy is what "you want" out of the divorce and your life after the divorce. Everything that is done by you and your legal team from here on out should have the ultimate purpose of getting you closer to getting what "you want" out of the divorce and setting you up to have the *Best Life* possible after the divorce.

Each time you face a decision about whether to take a contemplated action, you should be asking yourself: "Does this get me closer to my goals?" If the answer is "no," then you will both be wasting time and/or money and ultimately diverting yourself from having the *Best Life* possible after your divorce.

Once you have an understanding of your goals for the divorce (meaning you know what "you want") you need to meet with your divorce attorney to discuss and refine these goals. If you have not hired a divorce lawyer yet, you might be interested in the Bruce Law Firm's book , How to Find, Hire, & Work With

ASHLEY & CHRISTOPHER BRUCE
CONTROL YOUR DIFFICULT DIVORCE

Your Divorce Lawyer, which is available for free download at www.AllAboutDivorceLawyers.com.

Ideally, you should arrange to have an in-person meeting with your divorce lawyer shortly after you hire them. Then, in advance of the meeting, communicate to your lawyer that your purpose for the meeting is for them to understand your goals for the divorce, and to help you understand which of your goals are realistic, but also which of your goals are unlikely based on the law and the judges that may govern your divorce. Before the meeting, you should ask that your lawyer set aside the time to review the following documents, which you will provide in advance of the meeting with enough time for them to be read thoroughly:

1. Your written summary of your goals for the divorce (personal and financial), outstanding questions, potential negotiation leverage, and your marital history. If you have been using our forms, you would give the lawyer the Divorce Organizer document. It would be best if you updated this document to reflect any changes based on additional information learned about your situation or from the attorney interviews.

2. Your summary of the assets and liabilities subject to your divorce. If you are using our forms, this would be the Net Worth Organizer document.

3. Your current and after divorce budgets that you created for you and your spouse. If you are using our forms, this would be the Budget Organizer document(s).

4. Your summary of "questionable" or "suspicious" transactions. If you are using our forms, this would be the Questionable Transactions Organizer.

5. All of the financial and banking records you have gathered so far, as well as a list of anything that is missing, or you know exists and were unable to maintain.

When you meet with your lawyer, make sure that they understand not only your financial goals, but also your personal goals for how you want your life to improve after the divorce. Take advantage of the fact that your attorney has made a career out of helping people in your situation emerge from divorce so that they can life better lives. The attorney has likely had clients who have prospered during and after their divorce as well as those who have not done so well.

ASHLEY & CHRISTOPHER BRUCE
CONTROL YOUR DIFFICULT DIVORCE

Ask your attorney to give you their personal thoughts on whether "your head is in the right place" as to all of your goals for the divorce. Then, work with your lawyer to refine your goals to be both realistic and desirable. There is no sense setting goals for your divorce that cannot be reached, so make sure your goals are realistic.

We'd also suggest that you speak to a therapist/psychologist if you have not already to assist you with developing a set of non-financial goals for after the divorce. If you live in South Florida, you can go to our website, **www.StayMarriedFlorida.com**, for a listing of therapists in your area. If you have never been to a therapist before, you might be resistant to take this step, but having a plan to improve your life after the divorce that extends beyond a financial settlement is critical to you living the *Best Life* possible after your divorce.

You need to have a plan for the type of life that you want to live after the divorce. If you procrastinate addressing this aspect of your goal setting until after the divorce, you will be at risk of being worn-down, misdirected, and depressed, instead of energized, motivated, and optimistic once your divorce is over.

When you are done having these discussions with your lawyer and therapist and refining your goals, it would be optimal if you put your revised goals in writing, so that you can continue to remind yourself of the purpose of your divorce. Also, send the written version of your refined goals (both personal and financial) to your divorce lawyer, so they can stay focused on achieving your objectives through the "action plan" that is about to be created.

Develop Your Strategy

As soon as you and your divorce lawyer have collaborated to refine your goals, and have defined what is realistically achievable and in your best interests, it is time to work with your lawyer and therapist to develop your "strategy." Your "strategy" is how you turn goals and concepts into reality. It is the "big picture", an overview of what needs to happen before, during, and after your divorce lawsuit, for you to obtain your desired divorce settlement and the *Best Life* possible after your divorce. These strategies are the *Best Divorce* and *Best Life* strategies that we've referred to continuously throughout this book.

Some divorce lawyers are more inclined to focus only on developing an "action plan" for the legal aspects of your divorce. However, some lawyers (the best ones in our view) will incorporate the action plan from your therapist with your legal strategy, to allow you to see the results you're trying to achieve, and have the *Best Divorce possible* and the *Best Life possible* after the divorce. Our suggestion is to first develop your legal and personal "action plans" separately, and then to have them combined into one master "action plan."

The legal aspects of your "strategy" (which we call your *Best Divorce* strategy) should allow you to understand the order and timing of the items listed below, but might end up being more detailed:

1. **<u>What happens next?</u>** You need to know the next step in what happens now that you have hired your lawyer.

2. **<u>What needs to happen before the divorce lawsuit is filed</u>**? Are there any strategic initiatives that needs to be put in motion or completed before the lawsuit is filed? Are there any additional documents or evidence that needs to be gathered? Account access rights that needs to be terminated?

3. **<u>When will the divorce lawsuit be filed</u>**? Eventually, there will be a lawsuit for divorce filed with your name on it. At what stage of the process will this happen?

4. **<u>When will your spouse have to be notified about the divorce lawsuit</u>**? At a certain point, your spouse will be made aware that you intend to seek a divorce. You should know when this will happen as part of your planning. Note that there are separate chapters in Section #4 devoted to informing your spouse, children, and others about the divorce.

5. *When will negotiations with your spouse begin*? You should know the timeframe for when initial settlement negotiations with your spouse will start.

6. *What will be the initial settlement offer to your spouse*? You and your lawyer should define as much of your ideal settlement as possible. It may well be the case that you will need to obtain more information before you are in a position to define a complete settlement offer.

7. *What is your "drop dead" worst acceptable settlement*? You should work with your lawyer to define the minimum financial settlement acceptable to you to avoid taking your case to trial. You might not be able to define your "drop dead" settlement until you conduct financial discovery, and perform a net expected value analysis. See the chapter in Section 5 of this book titled *Utilizing a "Net Expected Value" Settlement Analysis* for a detailed explanation about how to do a net expected value analysis.

8. *What will need to happen in the litigation if your spouse refuses a reasonable settlement*? You need to understand what your lawyer plans to do if your spouse does not agree to settle your case on agreeable terms. Note Section

6 of this book details our philosophy on how to litigate a divorce case in a way that encourages the quickest resolution possible, regardless of whether there is a settlement or need for a judge to decide issues.

9. <u>**Are there any legal issues that will come up after the divorce is over**</u>? Depending on your situation there may be other issues that need to be addressed after the divorce. These can be as simple as updating your estate plan to complex tax planning and lawsuits involving the assets you received in the divorce. Either way, it is a good idea to know what these issues will be now.

As you get your legal *Best Divorce* strategy in place you also need to work with your therapist to come up with an "action plan" so that you are making progress towards your personal (non-financial) goals for your life after the divorce. Your personal improvement strategy (which we call your *Best Life* strategy) will be unique to you, but from our time spent counseling our clients, we believe your *Best Life* strategy needs to involve, at a minimum, the following components:

1. *<u>What happens next</u>*? Similar to your legal "action plan," you need to define the next step you need to take towards having the *Best Life* possible after your divorce.
2. *<u>What are you doing for you</u>*? What is your plan for reinvesting in yourself to make yourself a better, happier, person? What types of things do you want to do for yourself and when will you begin doing them?
3. *<u>What relationships will need to change</u>*? As you progress towards your life after the divorce, it is likely that the dynamics of some of your relationships with other people will need to change. As an example, if your spouse has historically threatened/controlled you, this needs to stop. You need to understand what changes will need to happen, how the changes will happen, and when the changes should happen.
4. *<u>What needs to happen with your social life</u>*? For some more than others, divorce brings about changes in social circles (relationships with friends). Sometimes, a *Best Life* strategy will need to involve creating, from scratch, a network of friends, as you might not have had many or any during the later parts of your marriage (this is not uncommon). You need to understand what types of

friends you want and have an agenda for developing these social relationships that starts now.

5. **<u>What will happen with your romantic/sex life</u>**? You should have an idea of how having another partner will fit into your foreseeable future along with what needs to happen before you are truly ready for a new relationship.

Developing your *Best Divorce* and *Best Life* strategies will put you well on your way towards having the *Best Divorce* and the *Best Life* you deserve after your divorce is done. You are just about ready to transition over from planning to action, but before you do, there are a few things you need to understand and have included in your *Best Divorce* and *Best Life* strategies.

Understand the Timeline of What Will Likely Happen & When

Divorce does not happen overnight. Neither does creating the life you deserve after the divorce. With this being the case, as you are developing your *Best Divorce* and *Best Divorce* strategies in collaboration with your lawyer and therapist, you need to develop a realistic understanding of when everything in your "action plan" will be happening.

One of the absolute worse things that can happen to you during your divorce or afterwards, is for you to all of a sudden become overwhelmed at how long it is taking to achieve your desired goals. If this happens, you will be tempted to give up and accept a result that falls short of your original goals out of a desire to end the uncomfortable experience.

When you do this in your divorce, you leave money on the table and in some cases, set yourself up for lifelong disaster by entering into support arrangements that put you in the poor house (this can happen both if you are paying or receiving spousal support). Perhaps even more unfortunate is "giving up" before you reach your *Best Life* goals for after the divorce. When this happens, you "settle" for a life less than you deserve, and risk falling right back into the habits that resulted in you seeking divorce in the first place.

In our experience, you will be far less likely to become overwhelmed and tempted to settle for less than your goals for both the divorce and your after-divorce life, if you develop an understanding now of how long it will take you to achieve your goals. When you know in advance how long everything is going to take then you will view the passage of time as a step closer to progress as opposed to a temptation to give up and fall short of your goals. Do yourself a favor and take the time now to work with your divorce lawyer and therapist to get a realistic understanding of how long it will take you to achieve your *Best Divorce* and *Best Life* after your divorce.

Understand Uncertainties & Possible Outcomes

For many people reading this book, there will be some initial uncertainties in the outcome of their *Best Divorce* and *Best Life* strategies. These uncertainties usually take the form of having incomplete financial information, wondering how your spouse will react to the divorce and behave in settlement negotiations, and wondering how a judge will rule upon "gray area" legal issues.

While we have included some strategies for handling these uncertainties below, you need to understand that there will always be uncertainties in your divorce up until the moment your divorce settlement or judgment is signed, and you will always face uncertainty in your personal life. The real key to dealing with these uncertainties is understanding now, while creating your *Best Divorce* and *Best Life* strategies, where the uncertainties exist. When uncertain outcomes are recognized upfront, you, your lawyer, and therapist can prepare for and account for the different possible outcomes in your *Best Divorce* and *Best Life* strategies.

ASHLEY & CHRISTOPHER BRUCE
CONTROL YOUR DIFFICULT DIVORCE

<u>*Uncertainty Caused by Lack of Financial Information*</u>:

A common form of uncertainty is caused by not having access to all of the financial information and statements needed to develop an accurate understanding of the marital assets, liabilities, income, and expenses. If your spouse historically controlled the important information then it's going to be harder, right now, to exactly understand what your goals for a divorce settlement should be. If this is you, don't worry.

Once your divorce case is filed, your divorce lawyer will be able to utilize numerous methods of obtaining the information that is needed to eliminate this uncertainty. For more on this, and an explanation of the process and timing of divorce, you might be interested in reading the Bruce Law Firm's Guide on Florida Divorce Law, which explains Florida's divorce laws and the legal process. The book is available for free download at www.FloridaDivorceLawGuide.com.

Furthermore, in most jurisdictions, your lawyer will be able to use their "subpoena power" to obtain information from other people or companies (such as accountants and financial institutions) to develop a more complete picture of the marital finances. Obtaining this information is one of the main components to the "Resolution Focused Litigation" philosophy we use in our practice and detail for you in Section #5 of this book.

Uncertainty About Your Spouse's Reaction & Behavior:

Another common uncertainty is how your spouse will react to the divorce and behave during the divorce. This includes whether your spouse will cooperate to agree upon an early settlement or act in a manner that "makes things difficult." In our experience, the best you can do to mitigate these types of uncertainties is to (1) take the time to plan out informing your spouse and other people about the divorce and (2) utilize a *Best Divorce* strategy that minimizes your spouse's ability to disrupt your divorce (this is a cornerstone to our "Resolution Focused Litigation" philosophy explained in Section 5 of this book). Otherwise, you need to recognize that divorce can be difficult, and your spouse might not be predictable. It might take some work to get out of your marriage and change your life for the better, and your spouse might not initially be the biggest fan of your decision to change your life.

On this point, we note that Section #4 of this book has separate chapters devoted to informing your spouse, children, and others about the divorce and dealing with your spouse during the divorce. Also, a great deal of Section #2, which covers the basics of leverage and strategy, explains concepts that can be worked into your *Best Divorce* strategy to mitigate disruptive behavior of an upset spouse. Also, in Section 4, the chapter titled *Finalize Preparations & Avoid Being "Cut Off,"* further addresses this issue.

Uncertainty About How the Court Will Determine Your Case:

Another form of common uncertainty involves not knowing how a judge will view the facts of your case and make a ruling. Especially on "gray area" issues or items that require the judge to believe one person over another. This type of "litigation uncertainty" is not common to divorce. Anyone who is involved in any type of lawsuit will deal with "litigation uncertainty." You should work with your lawyer to develop an understanding upfront of the potential outcomes in your case, especially on the issues that can go "either way."

Our typical approach to handling litigation uncertainty is covered in Section 5, the chapter titled *Utilizing a "Net Expected Value" Settlement Analysis*. The bottom line when it comes to litigation uncertainty is that your divorce lawyer needs to help you understand the potential outcomes for each "gray area" issue, and then help you understand both (1) the odds of each potential outcome and (2) the amount of money that will likely be spent pursuing the outcome. Once you know this information, it is possible to do several different calculations to make better sense of when it is appropriate (or foolish) to turn down a settlement offer.

Section 4: Move Forward & Avoid Distractions

**ASHLEY & CHRISTOPHER BRUCE
CONTROL YOUR DIFFICULT DIVORCE**

Your Life is Now Going to Get Better

You have taken the time to carefully determine that divorce is the best option for you. You know the basics of the law and process. You know what you want, and you've worked carefully to develop your *Best Divorce* & *Best Life* strategies. Now, it is time to put your plans into action and move forward. It is time to have the *Best Divorce* possible. It is time to move on to the better life you desire and deserve.

Thankfully, you've already been through about the worst of everything. Getting to this point in your marriage was probably not enjoyable. And for most people, there is not much joy in realizing and deciding that you need a divorce. From here on out though, things will change. Everything you will be doing will be focused on moving forward to have the *Best Life* possible. For the first time in a long time, you should be living a life filled with hope and optimism. This will be transformational. Your life is now going to get better.

What happens next is, your divorce lawyer will initiate the legal process needed to dissolve your marriage and resolve all related legal issues. As part of this process, your spouse and the children are going to be informed that the divorce is actually happening and eventually other people will find out too. Although you may not look forward to informing your spouse or children, or confronting friends, family, or colleagues, doing so is inevitable.

In the chapters that follow, we'll help you understand how to deal with announcing (and not announcing) your divorce to your family and others, and how to handle your spouse between now and when your experience with the legal system is complete. We'll also help you understand why it is important to cut out negative influences and "leave the law to the lawyers." You'll need to focus on moving forward with your *Best Life* strategy now, and not after the divorce.

Finalize Preparations & Avoid Being "Cut Off"

As you move forward it is important to be proactive to make sure that your spouse is unable to "cut off" your access to money or anything else that is important once they learn about the divorce. As explained in previous chapters in this book titled *Be the One to Control the Money & Documents* and *Do Not Create Short Term Cash Flow Problems*, you can be facing an "uphill battle" if the execution of your *Best Divorce* strategy is hampered by you running out of money or worrying about meeting your financial obligations. For this reason, your *Best Divorce* strategy may need to involve action items related to obtaining access to marital funds either before you file for divorce or early on in the litigation.

The proactive measures that can be taken to head off the impact of your spouse cutting you off depend in part on the laws in your jurisdiction and your specific situation, so you should ultimately defer to your divorce lawyer as to what can and should be done. That said, some of the commonly used strategies in Florida where we practice include:

1. <u>**Withdraw marital dollars and start a new account**</u>: A simple way to prevent cash flow problems is to withdraw

funds from a jointly titled banking or investment account and put the money in your own account at a separate financial institution. There is usually no law against moving your own money bank accounts and the transfer will have to be accounted for in the divorce. Taking this step can significantly reduce the work your lawyer might otherwise have to do to ensure you receive enough cash to pay for your living expenses. However, this step must usually be timed with the filing of your divorce case, because in many instances, your spouse can be quick to realize money has been transferred (especially if they receive text message or email notifications of significant transactions from their bank).

2. *Freeze financial accounts*: Another available "tool" for your lawyer depending on your jurisdiction is to "freeze" a financial account. In some cases, a temporary freeze can be achieved through filing a *"lis pendens"* on the account. The process of "freezing" a financial account can ultimately be used to assist with either a quick resolution of the entire divorce or as a way to facilitate getting you access to funds to use for your expenses during the

divorce litigation from an account that is only in your spouse's name.

3. *Change all account passwords*: Many problems can be mitigated by taking the steps explained in the chapter titled *Ensuring Your Privacy Part I: The Basics*, in the Bruce Law Firm's book, The Women's Guide to Getting Organized for Divorce, which is helpful to both men and women and is available for free download at www.GetOrganizedForDivorce.com. In any event, if you have a secure email address and change the passwords to all of your computers, devices, and online banking, email, and social media accounts you will substantially reduce the ways your spouse can cause you problems.

How to Tell Your Spouse About the Divorce

For many of our clients, telling their spouse about the divorce ends up being a liberating experience. Once your spouse is informed, you are able to focus on executing your *Best Divorce* and *Best Life* strategies and complete the "mental check out" from your unhappy marriage. All that is really left at this point with the divorce will be the legal work for the lawyers, which means you are largely freed up to continue following your carefully crafted plans to create the better life you desire and deserve.

But yes, at some point your spouse will need to be informed. And informing them is usually not an experience to get excited about. The process may not be pleasant, but it has to happen. The sooner it does, the sooner life starts to get better. The longer you wait to inform your spouse the longer you delay living the *Best Life* possible. Understood? Action is key. Action means progress. Hesitation means delay. Hesitation means more unhappiness. Don't hesitate with this or you will just disappoint yourself.

The most important things when it comes to informing your spouse about the divorce are (1) the method; (2) the timing; and (3) the word choice.

The Ways to Inform Your Spouse About the Divorce:

There are four primary ways that we instruct our clients to tell their spouse that they are getting divorced. These ways are:

1. The "direct method": You tell your spouse, face to face, that you are pursuing a divorce. In most cases, this is the best approach to utilize as long as there are not any anticipated domestic violence issues.

2. The "therapist approach": You inform your spouse, face to face, that you are getting divorced in the presence of a therapist (who should know in advance this will be happening). This approach can work well if you have been in counseling with your spouse, and you expect them to need extra emotional support when you inform them about the divorce.

3. The "attorney phone call approach": Your divorce lawyer will inform your spouse that you want a divorce (usually by a phone call). This approach is appropriate if you fear your spouse's reaction, if they are living in another geographic area, or you just want the divorce lawyer to have the difficult conversation for you.

4. The "process server approach": Your spouse is informed about the divorce by a process server finding them and serving them with divorce papers. Sometimes, this needs to be done to "send a message" for a strategic purpose involved with your *Best Divorce* strategy but in many cases this approach is not necessary or appropriate.

Overall, with most of our clients, the best method for informing their spouse about the divorce in terms of supporting an overall purpose of resolving legal issues on fair terms as soon as possible is to directly inform their spouse themselves (but see below on the timing of this). We find that the benefit of this is two-fold.

First, the "direct method" of having a face to face conversation is therapeutic for our clients. They realize divorce is really what they need in their life when they are able to stand in front of their spouse and tell them they are moving forward to dissolve their marriage. We find that our clients are more prone to "second thoughts" or "regret" about seeking a divorce when they use us or a process server to "break the news" to their spouse about the divorce.

ASHLEY & CHRISTOPHER BRUCE
CONTROL YOUR DIFFICULT DIVORCE

From my perspective, you should only pursue divorce when there is no other way for you to have the life you want to be living. If you are firm in the belief that there is no other path to your *Best Life* besides a divorce, you will not have a problem standing in front of your spouse and telling them that the marriage is over.

Second, the "direct method" of informing your spouse is also the most "direct method" of helping your spouse ultimately respect your decision to end the marriage and not hold a long-term grudge against you. In our experience, making the choice to be direct and honest with people will always get you more respect in the long run. In the context of divorce, this translates into higher odds of your spouse cooperating to resolve the legal issues on fair terms, as soon as possible, while minimizing collateral damage to your family and finances.

When your spouse learns about the divorce through other people, they are more prone to resent you for not being able to tell them directly (they'll say things like *"he/she didn't have the decency to tell me to my face"* when they are in their lawyer's office plotting world war three against you or trashing you to anyone who will listen). Also, they will be more likely to believe that you deep down really do not want the divorce, which can lead them to "litigate like a jackass" to make the divorce "hard for you" with the hopes that you'll realize you want to stay married in the process (we see this as one of the largest root causes of heavily litigated divorce cases).

The Best Timing for Informing Your Spouse About the Divorce:

As far as timing goes, in most situations, we advise our clients to hold off on saying anything to their spouse about the divorce until the point where the divorce lawsuit has already been filed. We usually take this approach because it assures that our client and law firm is moving forward (as opposed to "preparing to launch") when the other spouse is informed. Further, informing your spouse that you want a divorce <u>after</u> having already filed the lawsuit sends a clear message that you are serious and are moving forward, which puts your spouse in "reactive mode" and feeling like they are rushing to keep up with you. Creating this dynamic makes it much easier to settle your case on fair terms sooner rather than later. We've explained this in detail in Section 2 on the chapter titled *The First Mover Advantage (Move First, Unannounced, and Don't Back Off)*.

Word Choice When Telling Your Spouse About the Divorce:

ASHLEY & CHRISTOPHER BRUCE
CONTROL YOUR DIFFICULT DIVORCE

As to word choice, you should be direct, honest, and to the point when you tell your spouse that you want to dissolve your marriage. If you have already filed for divorce by this point, as we recommend, our suggestion is that you find an appropriate private time to speak to your spouse and tell them the following:

"After a lot of careful thought and reflection, I have made the decision to file for divorce. I have already hired a lawyer who has filed a divorce petition, so you will need to find an attorney. The lawyers will help us determine a fair and reasonable settlement. At this point, you either need to hire an attorney in the next couple of days who can receive the divorce papers, or I will arrange for my lawyer to send them to you directly if you determine that would make things easier."

Then, give your spouse the business card for your divorce lawyer, and say:

"This is the contact information for my divorce lawyer. He/she will be expecting to hear from you or your lawyer."

After saying these words, end the discussion, leave the room, and give your spouse some space.

Yes, there is probably a lot more than you could say during this conversation, but the bottom line is that the words will fall on deaf ears. You will have more time to explain yourself later. For now, tell your spouse what is written above and walk away. This might not be a bad time to have a pre-planned trip in place so that you can give your spouse (and yourself) some space.

How to Tell Your Children About the Divorce

You need to realize that a divorce is going to have an impact on your children forever. You would be well served to get professional help on this issue to make sure everything goes as well as possible with your children. Ideally, both you and your spouse will jointly consult with a children's therapist about how to inform the children about the divorce and then follow the therapist's recommendations for monitoring your children.

If you end up needing to inform the children before having engaged a therapist, you can, but be careful. Most of the experts suggest that parents jointly tell the children about the divorce. Whether the conversation is with your spouse or is only coming from you, it must be emphasized to the children that both parents love them and will continue to love them after the divorce. Make it clear up front that the divorce is not anyone's fault and was not caused by the children. This is extremely important because children tend to blame themselves for causing the family to break apart, even though there is not any reason for them doing so. Tell the children they will get to see both of their parents after the divorce, but eventually the parents will be living in separate homes,

where the children will each have their own bedroom.

As far as the reasons for the divorce, the experts suggest staying away from giving any specifics, although more details can be given depending on the age of the children. Further, you should avoid telling the children that the other spouse is to blame for the divorce.

Again, we want to emphasize that it is optimal to at least consult with a children's therapist about the best manner to inform your children about the divorce, and ideally you and your spouse should adopt a unified front when approaching the children.

Dealing with Family, Friends, & Colleagues

It is almost always the best strategy to keep your divorce as private as possible until after it is over. There is nothing to be gained by telling anyone about the divorce before it is over. Most friends and extended family (especially if they know and like both you and your spouse) would ultimately prefer to be kept out of your private situation unless you truly need their help. Otherwise, you should do everyone a favor and pay a therapist to give you advice about your personal life. Talking about your divorce to others can expose very private details that down the road you will probably wish you never told some people, especially if you change your mind and reconcile with your spouse.

When it comes to colleagues and business associates, you should almost always tell them nothing. Let them find out about the divorce after it is over from someone else. Otherwise, you put yourself at risk for others making unfair assumptions about your ability to perform in the workplace. Further, if you are in the process of negotiating any significant business deal, knowledge of your divorce can scuttle the entire thing as many people would prefer to do business with someone else instead of subjecting themselves and their company to subpoenas from divorce lawyers.

When confronted by friends, family, or coworkers / business associates about your divorce, the best course of action is to be honest about the issue and project an image of integrity and stability by saying something like:

"I am keeping this matter private. Everything is under control and we each have a lawyer helping us handle everything in a fair manner, so that there are minimal distractions for both of us. Out of respect for [name of your spouse] and our families, I am not going to talk about the divorce."

Sometimes, a spouse fears that their partner will go around and tell anyone who will listen about what a terrible person they are for ending the marriage and/or how they are trying to "take them to the cleaners"/ "take the children away"/ "ruin the family" or some other nonsensical story. If this is a possibility, and your spouse doing this will affect you living your *Best Life* after the divorce, then your *Best Divorce Strategy* may need to focus on an early settlement with enforceable confidentiality provisions.

Otherwise, it is best to take the high road in these situations. In most instances, people will equate your spouse's comments to them "just being upset" about the divorce. If people are really concerned about what your spouse is telling them, they will reach out to you. If this happens, it is best to say something like:

"I feel terrible that [name of your spouse] is not taking the divorce well. I know [he or she] will get through this, and it is not easy for me either. That said, I am keeping this matter private. Everything is under control and we each have a lawyer helping us handle everything in a fair manner so that our family can get through this. Out of respect for [name of your spouse] and our families, I'm going to stay away from discussing this further."

Remember that most people would rather be kept out of your divorce. If someone is alienated against you solely by what your spouse is saying, they would have taken your spouse's side anyway. There is nothing your spouse can do to alienate your good friends. If you stoop to the level of trashing your spouse or explaining the highly personal reasons for the divorce, the only thing you will accomplish is making yourself look unstable. This will cause you to be less respected by others in the long run when you want to be living the *Best Life* you deserve.

Handling Your Spouse During the Divorce

For most of you, one of the core reasons for pursuing the divorce is an undesirable relationship with your spouse. This should change beginning now. As your divorce unfolds, if you follow our advice, you will be setting the new dynamic for your ongoing relationship with your spouse.

The good part about all of this is that you can dictate the future relationship with your spouse by the way you handle them in the period of time between informing them about the divorce and the end of the legal proceedings/negotiations. If your spouse has historically been a controlling jerk, has always ruled you through their selfish demands, or has generally shown a lack of respect for you and your goals, you have the option of ending those relationship dynamics now.

Here is how:

1. **_Be Assertive but Don't Be a Jerk_**: You need to show that you, and only you, control your life from here on out. Nobody else will be telling you what to do or controlling your every move. You can do this by following your *Best*

Divorce strategy and pursuing your *Best Life* without hesitation or apology. When you do this, you will exude confidence. When your spouse sees you as a "man/woman on a mission" they will be less likely to get in your way. Obviously, this is all within reason. You do not want to be unreasonable/unrealistic in settlement negotiations or start acting like a jerk.

2. **<u>Stand Strong to "Boundary Testing"</u>**: Be aware that early on in the divorce your spouse might test the limits of how much they can control you, and the divorce process through you. This is especially the case if your spouse has historically displayed controlling or selfish tendencies. Usually these types of people don't change once a divorce starts, and they will rely upon what has previously allowed them to control/influence you during the marriage at the start of the divorce. These types of spouses will try to see if they can still control you early in the divorce through what is called "boundary testing." This boundary testing usually takes the form of your spouse trying to alter your behavior or provoke a reaction through their threats or demands.

The way to handle this "boundary testing" is to show your spouse that you are not going to be controlled. The sooner you stop reacting to your spouse's undesirable behavior, the sooner the behavior will end. This can be easier said than done, but if your *Best Life* involves you (and not your spouse) controlling your life, you need to stand up to "boundary testing." Preferably, your *Best Divorce* and *Best Life* strategies will have taken into account ways to minimize how your spouse can affect you through their behavior during the divorce.

3. **_Do Not Allow Your Spouse to Control Your Lawyer_**: One of the ways your spouse might attempt "boundary testing" is by trying to use you to control your lawyer to sabotage your legal strategy. We've made this into a separate point because of the potential disruption this will bring to your divorce. Do not get in the habit of having your lawyer make strategic case decisions based on instructions from your spouse. Please re-read the last sentence. Doesn't allowing your spouse to control *your* decisions and strategy seem a bit absurd (and maybe like the marriage you are trying to leave)? The whole point of developing your *Best Divorce* and *Best Life* strategies was to resolve

your divorce on fair terms, as soon as possible, with as minimal collateral damage to the family. When you start allowing your spouse to start altering this strategy then your divorce will likely take longer, cost more money, and ultimately cause more damage to the family. In most instances your spouse's short-term displeasure with your legal strategy will be far outweighed in the long run by a divorce that ends sooner and on fair terms.

4. *Handling Emotions*: You should not be your spouse's therapist during the divorce. You can try to occasionally give them confidence that they will also have a better life after the divorce, but that is it. If your spouse is continuing to use you as a shoulder to cry on you need to tell them to go to a therapist. Otherwise, you will continue to be your spouse's therapist after the divorce. Is that really what you want?

Similarly, you should keep your feelings about the divorce private, and avoid showing your spouse any signs of frustration or anger. You do not want to allow your spouse to see how the divorce might be hard for you, or any sign that you want the divorce to be over as soon as possible. Otherwise, your spouse might feel that you are "having second thoughts" and adopt a "settle nothing" litigation strategy out of hopes of you calling off the divorce if they make it "hard." Other spouses might sense your desperation and use it against you in settlement negotiations in an effort to get you to accept less money in a settlement.

Leave the Law to the Lawyer & Focus on Implementing Your Best Life Strategy

You are set up for success when you believe in your reasons for seeking the divorce, understand the basics of the law and the process, and have a *Best Divorce* strategy that puts you on the path to having the *Best Life* you desire and deserve. Still though, at times, the legal process of obtaining the divorce can seem overwhelming, emotional, or at least frustrating. Do not let this pull you away from pursuing your goals. As you are going through the actual legal process of the divorce, do not stray from implementing your *Best Life* strategy. You need to keep your positive momentum going. Avoid at all costs falling into the trap of putting your *Best Life* plan on hold "until after the divorce."

Sadly, the people who put implementation of their *Best Life* strategy on hold during the divorce are usually the people who never improve themselves after the divorce. You don't want to be one of these people. You deserve better. Do not trick yourself into believing that "you don't have enough time" or "it is too hard" to pursue your *Better Life* strategy until a judge signs a piece of paper that makes the end of your marriage official. Although the divorce might be occasionally frustrating and require a few meetings with your lawyer, the reality is that your actual involvement in the "legal process" should be minimal.

When you take the time upfront to gather information about your finances and "figure out what you want," all you should really be doing during the divorce litigation is occasionally answering your lawyer's questions and telling your lawyer whether you agree or disagree with settlement proposals. You are paying the lawyer to handle everything else. Be available to talk to your lawyer and check in when needed, but otherwise leave them to deal with the daily minutia of your divorce litigation.

You should take advantage of outsourcing the management and execution of your *Best Divorce* strategy to your lawyer and focus your efforts on following through to implement your *Best Life* strategy. Do not wait until after the divorce to do this. You should be starting now. If you feel like "there is not enough time in the day" to focus on yourself, you need to make yourself a priority and make the time.

Reread the chapter in Section #1 of this book titled: *Make Time for Yourself* if you are having trouble with creating the time you need to improve your life. Otherwise, you never will.

Avoid Negative Influences

This chapter is one of the shortest in the book but perhaps the most important.

If you find there are people who are getting in the way of you implementing your *Best Divorce* or *Best Life* strategies, you need to avoid them. Cut them out of your life. Block their phone number. Avoid them in social situations. Do what you need to do to surround yourself only with people who are supporting your goals. Anyone who is impeding your *Best Divorce* and *Best Life* strategies is hurting you. You've been hurt enough. Avoid these people at all costs.

When to Reassess Your Best Divorce & Best Life Strategies

A lot of thought should have gone into developing your *Best Divorce* and *Best Life* strategies with your lawyer and therapist. Keep in mind as you are moving forward that the best strategies for improving your life could be challenging to follow in the heat of the moment as you move through the difficult and life altering process that is divorce. However, in almost all cases, it is best to follow through on your *Best Divorce* and *Best Life* strategies and not "change course" midstream. Do not alter your game-plan for a better life just because it is the "easy way out."

That said, you have to remain flexible, and recognize that it will sometimes be necessary and optimal to change your *Best Divorce* or *Best Life* strategies. Once you start the divorce, your goals for settlement or your life after the divorce may change. You might realize that your intended path is producing unintended consequences. You also might realize you initially underestimated yourself, and you can and should do better.

Regardless of the reason, when it comes to reassessing your

ASHLEY & CHRISTOPHER BRUCE
CONTROL YOUR DIFFICULT DIVORCE

Best Divorce and *Best Life* strategies you need to make sure you are doing so for the right reasons, which your divorce lawyer and therapist will help you determine. Altering your strategy when doing so will make your divorce or life better. Do not alter your goals because it is "the easy way out." Having the *Best Divorce* to allow you to transition into your *Best Life* is not necessarily easy, but it will be worth it. You owe it to yourself to stay on track to improve your life.

Section 5: Resolution Focused Litigation

Your Litigation Strategy

In our view, you are wasting your time and money if your divorce lawyer does not put a plan of action in place that is designed to end your divorce on fair terms as soon as possible. If your spouse is not incentivized to settle on fair terms, you run the risk of your divorce litigation lasting far longer, then it should. When this happens, you will prolong your experience with a miserable situation and incrementally increase both the legal expenses of the divorce and the risk of the divorce permanently scarring your family.

The bottom line is your *Best Divorce* strategy has to be built around ending your divorce lawsuit on fair terms as soon as possible. Beyond the safety of our clients, this is the primary goal in our law practice. We accomplish this goal for our clients through a philosophy that we call "*Resolution Focused Litigation.*"

Do not be misled. *Resolution Focused Litigation* is <u>litigation</u>. Litigation means lawyers are taking action. This can be uncomfortable. But remember, divorce is not a comfortable or enjoyable situation for you. *Resolution Focused Litigation* is all about (often subtly) presenting your spouse with a situation that encourages them to accept a reasonable settlement offer so that your divorce can be over, and your focus can be completely freed to continue pursuing your *Best Life*.

In this section of the book, we first explain why *Resolution Focused Litigation* is necessary. Then, we will help you understand what *Resolution Focused Litigation* looks like in a typical divorce. Finally, we'll take you through how to utilize a logical formula for evaluating what your "bottom line settlement position" should be. By the end of this section, you will understand how to work with your attorney to resolve your divorce on fair terms at the earliest available opportunity. The only thing left for you to do will be to take action.

Why Resolution Focused Litigation is Necessary

Most people prefer to avoid confrontation at all costs and take the route of least resistance. It's natural to want to be the "nice guy" or "nice gal" and try to avoid anything involving conflict. This is especially true with divorce. For many, the first inclination in divorce is to attempt avoiding conflict by offering their spouse what they perceive to be a "fair" settlement to keep things "amicable" before any attorneys are involved.

Why complicate things when you can sit down at the dining room table with your spouse, discuss your differences, perhaps share a cry, and then figure out a settlement on the back of a napkin that one of you can take to an attorney to "make it legal." By doing it this way, you'll avoid subjecting your family to conflict and unnecessarily spending money on lawyers.

Nice try.

Unfortunately, this "extend the olive branch early" strategy rarely ever works when done as stated. Worse yet, despite the noble intentions, this type of divorce strategy almost always backfires and leads to the both people taking more time and money to resolve a sensitive situation that would otherwise be resolved quicker and with less conflict. Although counterintuitive, trying to mediate your divorce before lawyers, or with lawyers before a lawsuit is filed, almost usually always creates the conflict, delay, or expenses that almost everyone is trying to avoid.

The primary reason for this in most cases is there is a lack of a mutual, time-sensitive incentive for quick and rational divorce decision-making. Without a mutual desire for immediate divorce, there is no mutual cooperation towards an immediate divorce. Without lawyers being involved, there are no lawyer's expenses to avoid. Without any divorce lawsuit, there might not be any divorce to resolve/discuss. If your spouse sees no problems to solve from their point of view, then there are no problems that will be solved for your benefit.

Are you starting to see the problem? Sure, you have decided you'd like a quick, conflict free, *Best Divorce*. You know what you want and have carefully designed your *Best Divorce* and *Best Life* strategies to get what you want. All you need to do is sit down and work things out so that your family can move on in the best way possible. If this is you, we congratulate you on getting to where you're at now. Unfortunately, the process is hardly ever that simple. If your spouse does not agree with every single step of your new vision of taking half of the money and living a life without them (wouldn't that be nice?), this is likely not going to be simple and quick unless you have the proper incentives in place. This is where *"Resolution Focused Litigation"* becomes important.

You may have decided that divorce is the best option, but that took you a lot of time and soul searching. Your spouse is going to need to go through the same process. It is far easier to come to the conclusion that you are better off with a divorce on your own terms, then to learn how to cope with the news that your spouse wants divorce when you've never seriously contemplated the idea.

Some people ultimately realize that divorce is the best option, but this takes time. Your spouse will probably not be moving quickly. If they do, it will probably not be in any way you'll appreciate. There is the real reality that your spouse is going to feel hurt and make rash decisions out of fear or resentment. Sometimes, they will hire an aggressive lawyer and come out swinging. Other times they will shame your name to all your family, colleagues, and friends. There are endless possibilities.

ASHLEY & CHRISTOPHER BRUCE
CONTROL YOUR DIFFICULT DIVORCE

Although your spouse might deep down be trying to save the relationship, their actions can cause irreversible damage to your family, business/career, and other relationships.

Hopefully, none of these "doomsday predictions" will come true. But odds are, at the very least, your spouse is going to talk with their close friends and family. These people, some of whom have probably been through a difficult divorce themselves, are going to do what they can to watch out for your spouse. They will probably tell your spouse to be on guard and suspicious.

If the friends and family like you, they will still almost always tell your spouse to at least consult a lawyer to make sure they "know their rights." If the friends and family never liked you, were always "on the fence" about the marriage, or are jealous, there is no telling what they will encourage your spouse to do during their most vulnerable moments. Regardless, all of this will create the initial perception that you might be trying to "pull a fast one" with what you perceive to be a fair and reasonable settlement offer.

Most likely, there will end up being more investigation into the terms of your settlement offer that you made before lawyers, then if you had made the same offer during an active lawsuit, with lawyers, after exchanging the financial information that you will probably end up exchanging anyway. The shame to all of this besides the time delays and money wasted is you leaving the relationship feeling like you were being maliciously prosecuted and your spouse always thinking you got away with something. This type of divide can forever fracture the family unit and shared social circles. All because you were trying to do the right thing from the very beginning. The "no good deed goes unpunished" mantra seems especially applicable here.

So, is there a way to avoid all of this? A way to a dignified divorce that isn't like the *War of the Rosen's* story? Yes. It's what we call *"Resolution Focused Litigation."* Nearly all aspects of an amicable divorce you might desire are involved; but the "order of operations" is structured in a way that significantly decreases the likelihood of significant delays, unnecessary expenses, and feeling of resentment over the divorce with your spouse, friends, and family. All of this is concisely explained in the next chapter, *Resolution Focused Litigation Explained*.

Resolution Focused Litigation Explained

The most important thing we strive for as divorce lawyers is to end a complex divorce with a difficult spouse efficiently, as soon as realistically possible, and in a manner that preserves family relationships. So, how is this done? In many circumstances the best path to a quick and efficient solution to a difficult divorce is what we call *"Resolution Focused Litigation."* Resolution focused litigation involves creating an early incentive for your spouse to settle by simultaneously presenting a credible settlement offer and preparing a case to proceed to trial at the earliest available opportunity.

When employing this strategy, we often tell our clients they need to "prepare for trial to avoid trial." Why do we do this? Because it works to get divorces over sooner than they would otherwise be done for a lower net cost to marital finances and family relationships - plain and simple. We can hear you now saying "sure, if I pay more money to your law firm early on, you'll make all my problems go away…!" This isn't usually the case. You do not usually need to hemorrhage money and start a knock-down, drag-out, divorce war to resolve your legal issues. We named our litigation philosophy *"Resolution Focused Litigation"* because it is focused on **<u>Resolution</u>**.

The point is engaging in strategic litigation designed to incentivize an early settlement. In fact, putting forth a reasonable settlement proposal at the right time (and usually early on) is the cornerstone of my *Resolution Focused Litigation* philosophy. Further, as part of *Resolution Focused Litigation* you will not incur incremental legal expenses unless logic dictates the expense is worth the result. Almost always, the price you pay to your divorce lawyer to implement a *Resolution Focused Litigation* strategy will be dwarfed by the measurable financial damage and other disruption caused by lingering divorce.

So, what exactly does this resolution-based litigation strategy? Every case is different, but the general concept is to incentivize your spouse to accept a fair settlement early through a strategy that minimizes the damages delay brings you in divorce. This is usually done through taking the following actions:

1. **<u>File for divorce and "get things moving"</u>**: File the divorce lawsuit before confronting your spouse about the divorce and then provide as much financial disclosure to your spouse or their lawyer as soon as possible. Next, keep

things moving by setting your spouse's deposition to take place early on in the case after the exchange of the basic financial information, but far enough into the future to allow a real opportunity to settle your divorce lawsuit before the expenses of the deposition are incurred. If there are other key witnesses that would testify at trial for your spouse, then you may need to also start setting their depositions to take place at a time after you expect to be able to discuss a reasonable settlement offer. If experts need to be hired, such as forensic accountants, or vocational evaluators, these people will need to be retained now and your spouse should be made aware they are part of your team. Taking these steps now shows you are serious and doing what you have to do to win in court. Further, these are things you'll end up doing anyway if your spouse does not settle.

2. **_Exchange financial information and propose a reasonable settlement offer at the first opportunity_**: As soon as complete or reasonably complete financial information is available, you should provide it to your spouse along with a reasonable settlement offer. Then, schedule a mediation or settlement conference to discuss settlement options.

Ideally, this mediation or settlement conference is scheduled to take place close enough to the depositions, to create a sense of urgency in your spouse to settle, and avoid the depositions and associated expense -- but far enough before the depositions to make it unnecessary for your lawyers to incur the costs associated with preparing for the depositions if your case settles at the early conference or mediation.

3. *Make logical evaluations of settlement offers*: You need to make sure that you and your divorce lawyer work together to logically evaluate whether to accept or reject a settlement offer (or counteroffer) from your spouse. Usually, you should accept a settlement offer that is equal to or greater than what you'd receive in court minus all of the costs (lawyers, loss of income, etc.) to you of going to court. We've explained in detail how to do this evaluation in the chapter in this book titled *Utilizing a "Net Expected Value" Settlement Analysis*.

4. *Set a trial date as soon as possible*: Usually, one to two months after the divorce case is filed it is possible to obtain a trial date from your judge. In many jurisdictions, the trial date will be at least four to six months out, and sometimes

up to a year into the future. Also, to debunk a common misconception, there is usually not any "verdict" in divorce court at the end of trial. In nearly all jurisdictions, divorce trials are in front of one judge, who usually renders a written decision after the trial. Although many judges rule quickly, we've represented clients who have waited up to a year to receive their judge's decision. This means, from right now, it could take two years to end your divorce through the courts if things go quickly. In other words, the longer you wait to set a trial date the longer you delay this already lengthy and expensive process.

5. *Continue preparing for trial if settlement fails*: If there is no settlement at the early mediation or settlement conference, then continue preparing for the trial you have set while keeping a reasonable settlement offer on the table and adjusting it as necessary. Avoid the temptation to "cancel" or "reschedule" depositions to allow more time for settlement discussions, unless the delay is being caused by you providing incomplete information. There is no reason your spouse should need additional weeks or months to "think things through." This is almost always a stall tactic. If your spouse had any intention of ending

what is already an expensive and uncomfortable process, they would have settled. If your spouse will not agree to a reasonable settlement at an early mediation or settlement conference, the odds are that your spouse either: (1) will not settle until the last minute because they want to "ride out" their current situation (which might involve you paying all of their expenses) for as long as possible; (2) has not yet felt the financial pain of litigation to the point of realizing they need to settle; or (3) for whatever reason, they never intend to settle with you and are dead set on making you pay to finalize the divorce through the court system. In either scenario, the only right decision to resolve your case as efficiently and quickly as possible is to keep preparing for trial. Delay accomplishes nothing but more delay and spending more money.

The Costs of Delay

Most people prefer to avoid confrontation at all costs and prefer the route of least resistance. You are correct if you are thinking that *Resolution Focused Litigation* is going to create some attorney's fees and costs. However, these costs are initially minimal, as all that is really happening is a legal assistant in your lawyer's office will be taking time to schedule future events in your legal case. If your divorce settles, as many do when this strategy is employed, the majority of the costs associated with the depositions and a trial will never be incurred.

The real expense of divorce is the cost of delaying final settlement, especially if the delay is taking place while you are in litigation. These costs come in both quantifiable and non-quantifiable forms. As to the costs that can be counted, you'll find that in almost all situations, the financial effect of a lingering divorce is devastating. In many instances, a divorce involves one person paying for the expenses of two households from one set of income while also paying their lawyer, and maybe their spouse's lawyer. If you were looking for a way to blow through your savings quickly, this is it.

ASHLEY & CHRISTOPHER BRUCE
CONTROL YOUR DIFFICULT DIVORCE

Another large expense of the divorce that many initially underestimate is the effect the divorce has on the operation of a business, professional practice, or management of an investment portfolio. Any venture that requires you to perform at a high level is going to suffer based on the distractions of divorce. Some of the distractions will be time commitments. But the other, possibly most devastating distractions, include feeling like all of your hard work is going to be split with your spouse or that all of your decisions monitored and even second guessed by lawyers and forensic accountants. It's almost always true that eliminating these distractions correlates with you increasing performance and making more money.

Further, do not underestimate the cost that an ongoing divorce will bring to your family and friends. The longer your divorce lingers, the higher the potential for something to happen that creates irreversible damage. This is especially true with children, even when they are adults. For them, every part of your divorce that they are exposed to will create a lasting impact for them, and in their future relationships. We're not psychologists, but we tend to believe most psychologists would agree your family and friends are best off if you adopt our common-sense philosophy of implementing *Best Divorce* strategies designed to incentivize an early settlement or the fastest possible resolution through the courts if settlement is not reached.

Yes, a *Resolution Focused Litigation* strategy can initially subject both you and your spouse to what can feel like an adversarial environment. However, this period is brief, and is specifically designed to help you avoid the delays and confrontation that will cause irreversible damage to your relationships and finances. If you adopt a *Resolution Focused Litigation* strategy the odds are your spouse will quickly forget being briefly uncomfortable about your lawyer's legal assistant scheduling events that never ended up happening.

If your feel that your spouse will be forever resentful if you implement a *Resolution Focused Litigation* approach you need to, respectfully, wake up to reality. If your spouse is going to always hold a grudge at you for ending the marriage on fair terms as soon as possible, then they are the type of person who would have created far worse problems if you "extended the olive branch early" and before incentivizing them to accept a reasonable settlement. Sometimes in life, you have to choose between what can seem like two undesirable outcomes. This is probably one of those times. Choose the path likely to create minimal long-term damage.

Utilizing a "Net Expected Value" Settlement Analysis

Settling your divorce case can be tricky when "litigation uncertainty" exists. In other words, if it is not clear how a judge would decide a particular high dollar value issue in your divorce, it can be harder to determine what dollar value you should put on the issue in settlement negotiations. One way to handle this "litigation uncertainty" in a clear and logical manner is to have your lawyer perform a "net expected value" settlement analysis for any major items that you expect to negotiate with your spouse. Once you know the "net expected value" of a result, you can develop your *Best Divorce* strategy with the goal of obtaining at least the "net expected value" through settlement negotiations.

The steps to performing a "net expected value" settlement analysis are listed below. Don't worry if this seems a bit confusing at first as we close this chapter with an example of how to perform a net expected value analysis through a hypothetical example. For now, know that the steps to performing a net expected value analysis are:

Step #1: Determine the potential outcomes:

For issues where there is "litigation uncertainty," there will usually be at least two expected potential outcomes. For purposes of this analysis, an "outcome" is usually the result of a divorce court judge's decision. The first step in the net expected value analysis is determining the different ways the judge could see/decide a particular issue.

Step #2: Place a percentage on the likelihood of each outcome happening:

Have your lawyer tell you their estimated percentage probability of each potential outcome happening.

Step #3: Place a dollar value on each potential outcome:

This is the dollar value that you will receive or pay in each outcome scenario.

Step #4: Subtract the litigation and opportunity costs from the value to determine the "net value" of each potential outcome:

To get the "net value" of an outcome, you need to <u>subtract</u> the amount you will have to pay in attorney's fees and litigation costs from the amount of money you will be <u>receiving</u> in each potential outcome. You should also subtract the opportunity costs of litigation to get the real net value of each potential outcome.

NOTE: if a "potential outcome" involves you <u>paying</u> money instead of receiving money, then you need to <u>add</u> the attorney's fees, costs, and opportunity costs to the amount of money you will be paying in each potential outcome.

<u>Step #5: Multiply the net value of the outcome by the probability of it happening</u>:

For each potential outcome, multiply the percentage determined in step #2 by each "net value" determined in step #4.

<u>Step #6: Add up the sum of all of the potential probabilities</u>:

Add up the total of the result reached in step #5 for each potential outcome. This will give you the <u>net expected value</u>.

<u>Step #7: Determine the minimum acceptable settlement</u>:

ASHLEY & CHRISTOPHER BRUCE
CONTROL YOUR DIFFICULT DIVORCE

This part is easy! Your minimum acceptable settlement is the net expected value calculated in step #6. In other words, you should not accept a settlement for less than the total of the net expected

value of all of the ways a divorce court judge could decide the issue.

We'll give you a short and very basic example of how to make easy use out of what might at this point seem like a complicated concept.

Assume Jack and Jill are getting divorced. The big issue in the divorce is whether or not the judge will enforce a prenuptial agreement that Jack asked Jill to sign right before the wedding. If Jill convinces the judge to invalidate the prenuptial agreement, she will receive assets worth $1,000,000. However, if the prenuptial agreement stays in place, Jill will receive only $250,000. Jill's lawyer tells her that she has a 50% chance of having the prenuptial agreement invalidated by the judge, but she will need to spend $100,000 on attorney's fees to go through trial. Also, if Jill wants to litigate the issue, she will have to spend 10 days away from her medical practice, which will cost her $2,000 a day in lost profits, for a total of $20,000 lost profits.

To determine the minimum acceptable settlement offer based on these facts, go through the steps of the net expected value calculation:

Step #1: Determine the potential outcomes:

There are two potential outcomes: (1) the judge invalidates the prenuptial agreement or (2) the judge enforces the prenuptial agreement.

Step #2: Place a percentage on the likelihood of each outcome happening:

Jill's lawyer told her there is a 50% chance of each outcome.

Step #3: Place a dollar value on each potential outcome:

If the prenuptial agreement is invalidated Jill will receive $1,000,000 and if the agreement is enforced she will receive $250,000.

Step #4: Subtract the litigation and opportunity costs from the value to determine the "net value" of each potential outcome:

In either outcome, Jill will have to spend $100,000 on her lawyer and will lose $20,000 in revenue from her medical practice, for a total expense of $120,000. This means the net value to Jill of having the prenuptial agreement invalidated is $880,000 (($1,000,000 Jill receives by having the agreement set aside) – ($120,000 in litigation expenses and lost revenue) = **$880,000**). The net value to Jill if the prenuptial agreement is enforced is $130,000 (($250,000 received if the agreement is enforced) – ($120,000 in litigation expenses and lost revenue) = **$130,000**)

Step #5: Multiply the net value of the outcome by the probability of it happening:

In the case of the prenuptial agreement being invalidated, this is $880,000 x 50%= $440,000. In the case of the agreement being enforced, this is $130,000 x 50%= $65,000.

Step #6: Add up the sum of all of the potential probabilities:

The net value of the Jill's prenuptial agreement being invalidated ($440,000) plus the net value of the agreement being enforced ($65,000) equals a total net expected value to Jill of **$505,000**.

Step #7: Determine the minimum acceptable settlement:

Since Jill's net expected value of a litigation result is $505,000, if she were to follow the logic of the net expected value calculation, she would accept any settlement offer that was over $505,000.

The point to all of this math is to help you understand how to develop your *Best Divorce* strategy when facing "litigation uncertainty." If you were Jill in the example above, your *Best Divorce* strategy should be to developed around getting you at least $505,000 in a settlement (but hopefully more), with the understanding that it logically makes sense to go to trial and have a judge decide your case if Jack is offering less than $505,000 in a settlement.

We must make clear that evaluating what settlement to accept in order to avoid complex divorce litigation is not always going to be as simple as plugging numbers into a math formula. Usually, there are other variables that cannot be valued with a math formula that have to be taken into account. That said, a Net Expected Value analysis can be helpful for allowing you and your divorce lawyer to determine the "ballpark value" of your minimal acceptable settlement.

Section 6: Living Your Best Life After the Divorce

ASHLEY & CHRISTOPHER BRUCE
CONTROL YOUR DIFFICULT DIVORCE

Divorce is Only the Beginning!

Although it might seem unattainable, or like an eternity, sooner or later you will finalize your divorce and be ready to move on with your life. What comes next is my explanation of what you need to be doing after your divorce is over.

We could write an entire book on everything you need to be doing on continuing to move forward to have the *Best Life* possible after your divorce. In fact, maybe one day we will, but we need a break from getting up at 4:00 A.M. several mornings a week to write books for the time being. Fortunately, the basics of what you need to know moving forward are not very complicated.

The most important thing you need to remember is that there is no such thing as a "divorce miracle." A piece of paper signed by a judge dissolving your marriage may be a relief, but that piece of paper is not going to radically transform your life. Sure, you might finally be out of an unhappy, unhealthy, or unsatisfying marriage, but that is not where your story should end. Shouldn't your life story include more than just getting away from a problem? We think so. So should you. This is not the time to stop.

This is the time to keep moving forward. Your divorce is only the beginning of your progression towards a life you can enjoy living.

You might feel like "you just need a break," but you need to keep moving forward. Instead of slowing down, you need to ramp up your efforts of working towards your *Best Life*. Old habits are hard to shake. If you do not keep pushing ahead, you will substantially increase the odds of a "relapse" into a life or relationship that does not make you happy.

This is not any different than trying to lose weight. An overweight person will feel better about themselves and realize some health benefits after losing a few pounds. However, if the person does not continue to keep up a healthy diet and exercise lifestyle, the odds are that they'll gain back all the weight they lost. And more.

The point is, if you don't keep moving forward, you might end up right back in the same situation you just worked so hard to get out of, or something even worse. And this happens regardless of whether you eventually remarry or not. You do not want to allow yourself to become depressed and unhappy with a huge hole to crawl out of. Instead, you need to be focusing on moving forward to enjoy every day of your life. You need be focusing on living your *Best Life*.

If you have not worked with a therapist yet, we highly recommend you see one at this point for purposes of working on your plan for continuing to improve your life after the divorce. You can go to **www.StayMarriedFlorida.com** to see a list of some great therapists if you live in the Florida area.

Best Life Action Items

We are by no means therapists or in a position to tell you what should be the goals of your life after your divorce. That said, our business is mostly limited to breaking up our clients' marriages and dealing with legal issues that come up after a divorce, so we'd like to think we have some insight into what can allow you to be happy when your divorce is over. So, for what it is worth, we have come up with a list of "action items" that you might consider incorporating into your *Best Life* strategy for after the divorce:

<u>Get away for a while</u>:

If you can, you should clear your schedule and get out of town for a week (or more). Visit somewhere you've always wanted to go and do something you've always wanted to do. Taking a break to clear your head will help you reflect on what should be happening next in life. Also, crossing a dream vacation off your bucket list will be motivating for you in terms of continuing to build the life you want for yourself.

<u>Spend time on the things that make you happy</u>:

Do what you love and you'll love what you do. We realize this

saying sounds cliché, but it could not be more true. You might not have a lot of free time or the ability to instantly reinvent your business or career, but take the time you do have for yourself to do the things you love to do.

<u>Prioritize your needs</u>:

During your marriage, you may have always been putting other people's needs above yours, or maybe you just did not ever have enough time to focus on yourself. For you to continue to improve your life, you need to start making yourself a priority. Prioritize your needs over the needs of other people and make the time to pay attention to yourself. We're not advocating being selfish. What we're suggesting is you start making the time to do something for yourself. You don't have to do anything drastic, but we find that our clients who do little things like creating a few hours a week to exercise, take a class, or pursue a hobby/interest, are almost always happier and more successful in the long run. For more information on this, you should re-read Section #1 of this book, specifically the chapter titled *Make Time for Yourself*.

Have a plan:

Face it. If being happy and living the life you always wanted was simple, then you would not have experienced a failed marriage or picked up this book. Also, statistically speaking, the fact that your first marriage ended in divorce makes in even more likely that a second marriage will end in divorce too. But enough about statistics because you are not going to be one. When you realize that you need a basic plan for your divorce recovery and future life, <u>and take the time to make and follow that plan</u>, you will be on track for having the so called *Best Life* that we keep talking about in this book. Hopefully you've already developed what we call a *Best Life* strategy. But if not, go back and read *Step #7* of this book.

Get support:

Possibly more important than having a plan for your divorce recovery and future life, is having a person or people to help you develop that plan and hold you accountable to it. We recommend you get professional help with this and hire a no-nonsense therapist who can help you develop your *Best Life* strategy and hold you accountable to your progress. The reason we recommend you hire a therapist is because by doing so, you can avoid having to share personal details with friends and family that you might one day realize you would have rather kept private. Also, experienced therapists have previously helped many people in your situation move on from their divorce to pursue and achieve their *Best Life*.

For some reason, certain people are averse to seeing therapists. They think seeing a therapist requires a mental health disorder or that therapists waste time or are too "touchy feely" to make a difference in their life. Ironically, many of these people are the same people who will eagerly pay top dollar for professional advice when it comes to running and optimizing their businesses. This is nonsense. There are plenty of great results-driven therapists. Go see one so you can optimize your personal life like you optimize your business or professional life.

<u>**Make and keep healthy habits**</u>:

If you are not doing so already you need to make sure you are making healthy choices. Try to eat right, exercise regularly, and avoid alcohol and substance dependency problems. You do not need to obsessively count calories, live inside a gym, or live like a saint, but you should make sure that you are generally living a healthy lifestyle. Think of it this way: going to all of the trouble of developing and executing upon *Best Divorce* and *Best Life* strategies will not do you any good if you are dead.

Do not avoid or obsess over new relationships:

With some of our clients, it seems like they either avoid new relationships completely or are obsessed with having new relationships. Relax. First off, if you are ever going to live your *Best Life*, you will need to realize that it starts with you and does not require anyone else. You can be a very happy person without being married or immediately dating someone else. If you are having trouble realizing this, or have pervasive fears of being alone, then you need to see a therapist immediately. Just as you should avoid being obsessed with immediately jumping into a new relationship, you should not rely on the "I never want to get married again" attitude to avoid new relationships.

When it comes to dating after the divorce, our advice is to do what comes naturally. If you make the time to participate in activities that make you happy and get out around other people, then your new relationships will usually come with time, and at the right time. And if you are worried about getting remarried, remember that just because you are dating someone does not mean you need to get married to them. Also, you can avoid nearly all of the problems and hassle of a divorce if you take the time to get a solid prenuptial agreement, so you should not necessarily be avoiding marriage like the plague anyway.

Dealing with Your Former Spouse After the Divorce

Our advice for handling your now former spouse after the divorce depends on whether you have any children together or any ongoing financial commitments to each other after the divorce.

If you do not have any children, or do not have to deal with each other in the future over payment/receipt of support or financial matters, then our thoughts are that you should cut off all communication to your former spouse and interactions with your former spouse. There is not going to be anything good to come by interacting with them.

Your efforts to rebuild from the divorce and pursue your *Best Life* will be seriously set back if you reinitiate contact (especially sexual relations) with your former spouse. Even if you have successfully "moved on" from the marriage, you need to remember that things may be different for your former spouse. If they did not want the divorce, and might not yet be "over you," then it is not fair to them for you to be in contact with them. Doing so sends mixed signals, which makes it harder for your former spouse to recover from the divorce. Further, your contact with a former spouse might make them think "there is still hope" for the relationship, which can result in stalking and other fallout that can come with them trying to "get you back." None of this is good, and there is nothing to be otherwise gained by you contacting your former spouse.

If you are reading this while still married and think our "cut all ties" advice sounds "undoable," this might be a sign that you should not get divorced. Try to take another shot at couples' counseling to see if your marriage can be turned around or try individual counseling to help you understand your feelings and whether divorce is really the best option for you.

If you have children, then you are going to need to get along with your spouse and communicate with them on children's issues. This is true regardless of whether your children are young or are adults living out of the house. For your children, whether they admit it or not, it will be very important to them that you and your former spouse are able to present a unified front on parenting issues, and get along at family gatherings, both when the children are young and when they are adults.

You need to realize that if you and your spouse cannot get along, your children will bring your conflict into their life and future relationships. Worse yet, the animosity might result in them withdrawing from both parents, and will make them more prone to being programmed to think that it is acceptable for parents to routinely fight about children (it is not).

The bottom line is that if you have children, you need to "suck it up" and learn how to get along, even if this means you have to keep your thoughts to yourself every now and then. Do keep in mind that your ability to "get along" with your former spouse is probably going to improve with time. Everything usually gets better once both former spouses move on from the divorce. Also, if there are challenges in your interactions with your former spouse, you should consider several sessions of family counseling for purposes of improving relationships. Sometimes, one or two sit down meetings with a neutral person can make a world of a difference in improving interactions. This is worth doing for the sake of your children.

If there are no children, but there are ongoing financial commitments, you will benefit long term from having a cordial relationship with your spouse. It should go without saying that if you are depending on your spouse to pay your ongoing financial support, then it is not helpful to be nasty or disrespectful. The same goes if you are the person paying support. One day, you might have issues come up that require your spouse to "ease up" or "cut you a break" if you have financial problems. It is much easier to get some sympathy from your former spouse down the line if you treat them with respect at all times.

ASHLEY & CHRISTOPHER BRUCE
CONTROL YOUR DIFFICULT DIVORCE

Stay Out of Divorce Court!

As much as we love what we do and value the services we provide as divorce lawyers, it is hard for us to think of many examples of how your life would be improved after the divorce if you spent more time in divorce court. Although divorce is difficult and usually an experience to try to avoid repeating, we are still continually amazed at how many people end up rehiring lawyers to fight with their spouse after the divorce. Believe it or not, typically 25-40% of our law practice is dealing with clients who are litigating with their spouse after their divorce has already been finalized.

So, as final parting words of advice, and at risk of reducing the income of our law practice, we'll give you our top five no-brainer ways to stay out of divorce court once your divorce is over:

1. <u>*Follow your settlement agreement or court order*</u>: Your divorce was either resolved through a settlement agreement with your spouse or a judge setting the terms through a court order. Either way, you need to follow that agreement or order. Following the order is mandatory,

not optional. When you don't follow the settlement agreement or court order you make it more likely that your former spouse will retaliate, and you open yourself up to sanctions, which can include incarceration. In some cases, it is possible to modify portions of your settlement, especially with spousal support, but unless your agreement is modified it needs to be followed.

2. <u>**Keep things civil with your former spouse**</u>: We believe the root cause of most post-divorce family court litigation is fallout over an argument or incident between former spouses involving one embarrassing the other. You don't need to be your former spouse's best friend; but don't be nasty or do something that would embarrass them. Also, it is generally not helpful to rub new relationships or your post-divorce success in your former spouse's face. Basically, if you're not a jerk, you'll be fine. We've laid out how to deal with your former spouse in a later chapter titled *Dealing with Your Former Spouse After the Divorce*.

3. <u>**Learn how to have healthy future relationships**</u>: You need to learn how to have healthy future relationships so that you avoid going through the divorce experience with

another person in the future. Although we're not therapists, we believe we're probably more qualified than most people to give an opinion on why marriages fail. Based on what our clients tell us and what we observe, most marriages fail because there is a lack of communication between spouses as to how they want to be loved. This results, over time, in one or both spouses feeling like their needs are not being met. Eventually, the marriage ends up drifting apart. Don't let this happen to you (again). You should read the book *"The Five Love Languages"* by Dr. Gary Chapman, which concisely explains in layman's terms how to meet the needs of your spouse or partner. We tolerated the book, and we are not naturally touchy-feely people. If we can get through the book so can you. We especially recommend the audiobook version. The reader has an entertaining southern accent that we would not normally associate with someone reading a book about relationship advice.

4. **_Avoid relationships with unstable people or people with personality disorders_**: Some relationships are destined to fail from the beginning because the other person is a hot mess or has a personality disorder. If you want to avoid

another failed relationship, avoid dating people who will drive you crazy or make you hate them in the long-term. Dating or marrying someone because you want to "save them" or think you can "change them" never works (unless you change yourself and adapt to being miserable). If they are a crazy mess when the relationship starts it is only getting worse. With few exceptions, generally people who have lived in more than three cities or have had more than three job changes in the last two years are unstable. Also, you might be dating a legitimate psychopath if they cheat on their tax returns; have extreme "hot" and "cold" attitudes towards you; jokingly put you or your friends/family down; or subject you to an extremely fast "whirlwind" courtship. Life is too short to be spent with someone who lacks stability or has a personality disorder. Don't do it!

5. <u>**Get a prenuptial agreement**</u>: Next time, get a prenuptial agreement! The best *Best Divorce* strategy is to avoid divorce. The second-best *Best Divorce* strategy is to resolve your divorce before you get married. You can do this through a prenuptial agreement. Just make sure to follow all of the rules in your jurisdiction when entering into a

prenuptial agreement. If you get sloppy or cheap with these agreements, they can be worthless or create more problems than they solve. Usually, it is best to make sure that (1) both people have lawyers; (2) the agreement is signed at least a month before the wedding; (3) thorough financial disclosure is given; and (4) the signing of the agreement is taped and recorded, with it being made obvious that both people are sober, understand the agreement, and want to sign it.

Our Other Books Designed to Help You

Hopefully you have found this book helpful to you in your time of need. In case you were looking to learn more, we wanted to make sure you knew that this is not the Bruce Law Firm's only book.

The Bruce Law Firm has several books available for free download at www.DivorceInformationBooks.com. These books are free and include this Divorce Strategy Guide, the Florida Divorce Law Guide, the Women's Guide to Getting Organized for Divorce, our guide on How to Find, Hire, & Work With Your Divorce Lawyer, and How to Divorce Your Controlling, Manipulative, Narcissistic Husband.

Also, because it is our belief that the real best divorce is the divorce that didn't have to happen, the Bruce Law Firm developed and supports www.StayMarriedFlorida.com, a website devoted to helping couples build, have, and keep healthy relationships. The website has articles, podcast interviews, and a growing directory of extremely talented results-driven therapists.

If you found this free book helpful, the best compliment you could give would be to share our books with others who might be in need (just direct them to www.DivorceInformationBooks.com). Also, we love it when people spread the word about the Bruce Law Firm on Avvo.com (google Christopher R. Bruce Avvo and Ashley D Bruce Avvo and click to leave a review) or our google business page (google Bruce Law Firm West Palm Beach and click the link to leave a google review).

ABOUT THE AUTHORS

Ashley D. Bruce is a divorce lawyer in West Palm Beach and Wellington, Florida. She got her start in divorce from her mother, Bernice Alden Dillman, who practiced divorce and family law for over thirty years in Boca Raton. Growing up Ashley often witnessed clients walk into her mother's office on the first day, distraught, insecure, and upset, and watched them blossom into being more confident, secure, and their knowing that a better life was ahead. Watching her mom guide clients through this transformation helped Ashley realize that she, too, wanted to help clients grow and have a better life.

Ashley's early experience shadowing her mother and handling complex business litigation and bankruptcy law (she did a lot of "bet the company" litigation and cases involving financial fraud) was an outstanding platform for the focus of her current law practice, which is handling "the harder" (some might say nasty) divorce and family law cases where something very important or valuable is often at issue.

In all cases, Ashley's goal is to obtain a favorable result for clients as quickly and efficiently as possible so they can move on to the life they desire and deserve to be living. She strongly believes in resolution focused and strategic litigation (which means that she will counsel a client to litigate when it needs to be done, for example to align an unruly spouse more with legal reality when they are taking a ridiculous position) but believes resolving matters out of court is usually in the best interest of the clients, not only financially, but also psychologically.

Outside of the office, and spending time with our young children, Ashley's passion is animal rescue, and trying to make the world a better place with kindness to animals. Ashley also enjoys horseback riding, mountain biking, snowboarding, tennis, photography, theater, and a variety of other activities. Ashley is married to Christopher R. Bruce, and can be reached at (561) 810-0170 or abruce@brucepa.com.

Christopher R. Bruce is a divorce lawyer and appellate lawyer for divorce cases and has been for nearly all of his legal career and he is a Florida Bar Board Certified Marital & Family Law Specialist. His law practice is predominately limited to representing his South Florida clients in divorce and family court matters involving business valuation and asset tracing issues, the need to confront a difficult or intimidating person, the prosecution or defense of long-term financial support claims, or serious issues involving children.

Chris takes a particular interest in representing women in divorces from narcissistic or emotionally abusive/manipulative husbands. This is because Chris feels these cases are most likely to result in his client having a dramatically improved and transformed-for-the-better life once the divorce is over.

Chris founded the Bruce Law Firm, P.A. in November 2016 and the multi-lawyer law firm is limited to divorce and family law matters.

Chris is a native of Palm Beach County, Florida, and a graduate of Palm Beach Gardens High School. Outside of the office, and spending time with his family, his passion is saltwater fishing and marine conservation. Chris enjoys participating in South Florida billfish tournaments and promoting marine species and habitat conservation.

Chris frequently publishes articles on current topics in Florida Divorce Law, and serves as a resource to news agencies reporting on Florida divorce issues. His articles have appeared in the *South Florida Daily Business Review, Palm Beach County Bar Bulletin* and several other Florida Bar publications.

A proponent of keeping families together, Chris developed **www.StayMarriedFlorida.com**, a resource for helping people build, have, and keep happy and healthy relationships.

Chris developed **www.BrucePA.com** to further help people create the best probability for making their divorce a *"Best Divorce"* that allows them to move on to a life to be proud of when their divorce is over. The website's resources include complementary books, seminars, and forums on divorce strategy, law, and procedure.

If you would like to contact Chris in regard to appearing on StayMarriedFlorida.com, a Florida divorce or family law matter, this book, or anything else, you can call (561) 810-0170 or send an email to cbruce@brucepa.com.